America's Best
QUILTING
PROJECTS

Edited by Karen Costello Soltys
Written by Marianne Fons and Liz Porter

Special Feature
STAR QUILTS

Rodale Press
Emmaus, Pennsylvania

Our Mission

We publish books that empower people's lives.

RODALE BOOKS

America's Best Quilting Projects
Editorial and Design Staff
Editor: KAREN COSTELLO SOLTYS
Technical Writers: MARIANNE FONS AND LIZ PORTER
Cover and Book Designer: DENISE M. SHADE
Book Layout: ROBIN M. HEPLER AND LISA PALMER
Photographer: MITCH MANDEL
Photo Stylist: MARIANNE G. LAUBACH
Project Illustrator: SANDY FREEMAN
Tips and Techniques Illustrator: CHARLES METZ
Logo Designer: SANDY FREEMAN
Copy Editor: ANN SNYDER
Administrative Assistant: SUSAN NICKOL
Production Coordinator: MELINDA RIZZO

Rodale Books
Executive Editor, Home and Garden:
  MARGARET LYDIC BALITAS
Managing Editor, Quilt Books:
  SUZANNE NELSON
Art Director, Home and Garden:
  MICHAEL MANDARANO
Copy Manager, Home and Garden:
  DOLORES PLIKAITIS
Office Manager, Home and Garden:
  KAREN EARL-BRAYMER
Editor-in-Chief: WILLIAM GOTTLIEB

On the Cover: The quilt shown is Old Schoolhouse and may be found on page 90. The fabric shown is Stars and Stripes, pattern number III-TN, by P & B Textiles. Antiques are courtesy of Lynn Carpenter and Andrea Costello, Harleysville, Pennsylvania.

Photography Location: The photographs in this book were shot at the Joseph Ambler Inn, Horsham, Pennsylvania.

The editors who compiled this book have tried to make all of the contents as accurate and as correct as possible. Illustrations, photographs, and text have all been carefully checked and cross-checked. However, due to the variability of materials, personal skill, and so on, Rodale Press does not assume any responsibility for any damages or other losses incurred that result from the material presented herein. All instructions and diagrams should be carefully studied and clearly understood before beginning any project.

If you have any questions or comments concerning this book, please write to:
  Rodale Press, Inc.
  Book Readers' Service
  33 East Minor Street
  Emmaus, PA 18098

Library of Congress Cataloging-in-Publication Data

Fons, Marianne.
    America's best quilting projects : special feature star quilts / edited by Karen Costello Soltys ; written by Marianne Fons and Liz Porter.
        p.   cm.
    ISBN 0–87596–642–X hardcover
    1. Quilting—Patterns. 2. Patchwork—Patterns.
3. Stars in art. I. Porter, Liz. II. Soltys, Karen Costello. III. Title.

TT835.F643 1995
746.46—dc20   94–23049
                                                CIP

Distributed in the book trade by St. Martin's Press

2 4 6 8 10 9 7 5 3   hardcover

Contents

Acknowledgments

Gemstones by Jeanne Jenzano, Alden, Pennsylvania. Jeanne is a member of two quilt guilds, Undercover Quilters and Main Line Quilters. She loves scrap quilts because she is always amazed that so many different fabrics can work so well together. Jeanne pieced Gemstones in jewel-tone scraps for a wedding gift for her son and daughter-in-law. Gemstones won third place in the Undercover Quilt Show in 1993 and was also selected as a juried quilt in the 1993 Quilters' Heritage Celebration.

Let It Grow by Sue Nickels, Ann Arbor, Michigan. Sue is a quilting teacher, guild member, and award-winning quilter. Her Let It Grow design was inspired by a workshop with Gwen Marston as well as by an antique quilt in the collection of Michigan State University. She uses this quilt as a class project for her machine appliqué classes. Let It Grow was honored with first place in appliqué at her guild's yearly challenge and was selected for exhibition for the 1992 International/American Quilt Festival in Houston.

Baskets of Love by Connie Rodman, West Fargo, North Dakota. Connie joined the Quilters' Guild of North Dakota in 1986 at the urging of her aunt. She thought she'd have nothing in common with a bunch of quilters but soon found that she fit right in. In fact, it was her quilt guild that pieced the baskets in this quilt. Baskets of Love won both the Guild Award and the Teacher's Award at her guild's 1991 Indian Summer Quilt Show. Connie is also a member of a smaller quilt group, Designing Quilters, which promotes quilt shows at local galleries.

Overwhelmed by Autumn by Diane Doro, Des Moines, Iowa. Diane made her first quilt 14 years ago but didn't seriously begin quilting until 1988. Her favorite quilts have a three-dimensional quality and high contrasts in color and values. Overwhelmed by Autumn was most recently displayed at the Des Moines Area Quilters' Guild's Tenth

Anniversary Quilt Show. Diane is a member of the guild and has coordinated the making of raffle quilts for two of the guild's annual shows.

Great-Grandma Goebel's Bridal Quilt by Elsie Campbell, Arkansas City, Kansas. Elsie has been stitching since the age of three, yet it wasn't until 1987 that she became a dedicated quilter. She is a member and pattern chairwoman of the Walnut Valley Quilters' Guild. Elsie's rendition of her Great-Grandma Goebel's Bridal Quilt was one of several chosen for full display at the 1993 Silver Dollar City's National Quilt Festival in Branson, Missouri, and has been displayed alongside the original quilt in her guild's 1994 annual show. It was also selected for show at the American Quilter's Society's 1994 15th Anniversary Show.

Bringing Lilies to the Table by Adrienne-Joy Chiet, Wellington, Florida. In 1986, Adrienne-Joy's husband bought her a sewing machine, she copied a tulip quilt from a cookbook, and she has never looked back. She traveled to the International Quilt Festival in Houston, promptly returned to her home in New York where she converted all her needlework friends to quilters, and then moved to Florida where she is still busy stitching and quilting. Bringing Lilies to the Table was made specifically for the national Labor of Love contest. It was selected as first runner-up in her local quilt shop and was displayed at the 1993 show in Houston.

Duck Quilt by Teresa S. Hannaway, Lafayette, Colorado. Teresa has worked both as a designer and as a photo stylist for The Needlecraft Shop. Since moving to Colorado, she has become a freelance designer for various needlecrafts including sewing, quilting, crochet, and general crafts. Her designs have been published in several magazines, but this Duck Quilt is exclusive to *America's Best Quilting Projects*.

Tulips 'Round the Garden Path by Barbara Hammett, Tulsa, Oklahoma. Barbara is a prolific quil-

ter who began quilting in 1985 and has completed over 65 quilts to date. She made this quilt in a class taught at The Cotton Patch, a quilt shop in Tulsa, and based the pattern on a design by Betty Terrill. Barbara's pastel rendition of this quilt was displayed at the 1993 Quilters' Heritage Celebration in Lancaster, Pennsylvania, as well as at the 1990 Tulsa State Fair where it won first place in the mixed technique category. Tulips 'Round the Garden Path also won second place in the innovative pieced bed category at the 1991 Green Country Quilters' Guild Quilt Show in Tulsa.

Patchwork Needle Case by Kathy Berschneider, Rockford, Illinois. Kathy works as a computer aide at a local elementary school and looks forward to the relaxation sewing and quilting provide at the end of the workday. She has also taught classes, clerked, and made display items at a local quilt shop. Since she always seemed to be looking for the newest idea and latest patterns, Kathy decided to try her hand at designing her own projects, and shares this needle case design exclusively with *America's Best Quilting Projects*.

Oak Leaf and Reel by Melva Betka, Rankin, Illinois. Melva's adaptation of the Oak Leaf and Reel quilt published in 1988 in *Quilters' Newsletter Magazine* boasts of her own oak leaf and acorn quilting designs. In fact, Melva just loves to quilt, adding lots and lots of small, even stitches. Her beautiful quilt was discovered at the Quilts Across America 1992 show in Peoria, Illinois.

Pisces by Joann Dixon, Fairbanks, Alaska. Joann selected a traditional Milky Way block design for her quilt, added batik and hand-dyed solids, and quilted her project from the back side. Her quilting is influenced greatly by fabrics—especially batiks—and by Kumiko Sudo, author of *East Quilts West*. Joann is an active member of her local quilt guild, Cabin Fever Quilters. Pisces was begun at her guild's annual Quilting in the

Snow retreat and won second place in the 1993 Labor of Love contest and was displayed at the national show in Houston.

California Star by Bobbi Finley, San Jose, California. Bobbi's hand-pieced and hand-quilted masterpiece has been displayed and juried in three prominent quilt shows: the International Quilt Festival in 1992, and the Pacific International Quilt Festival and the American Quilter's Society National Quilt Show in 1993. Bobbi started quilting when she first began noticing antique quilts and decided she wanted to learn how to make them.

Fantasy Remembered by Joyce Stewart, Rexburg, Idaho. Joyce's winning quilt was discovered when it was part of the Hoffman Challenge display in 1992 at the International/American Quilt Festival in Houston. Joyce is an avid quilter and teacher and, along with her sister, taught classes for the first time at the American Quilter's Society Show in Paducah, Kentucky, in 1994.

Moon and Stars by Sara Hedrick, Vacaville, California. Moon and Stars is Sara's very first quilt, begun in San Diego and completed two and a half years later in the San Francisco Bay area. She designed the quilting pattern herself and has since moved on to lots of new quilting projects—one for each new grandchild, all completed in time for their first birthday.

Old Schoolhouse by Norma Grasse, Perkasie, Pennsylvania. Norma, a charter member of the Variable Star Quilters, is a collector of old fabrics. She put her antique black and red fabrics to good use in this unique adaptation of the traditional schoolhouse quilt. Norma also used an antique template for the star flowers (or pinwheels) in the border. Old Schoolhouse was displayed at the 1993 Quilters' Heritage Celebration in Lancaster, Pennsylvania.

Midnight Starburst by Carla Moore, Oklahoma City, Oklahoma. Carla decided to make a baby quilt after seeing a quilting show on television. When her mother commented that she thought the stitches were supposed to be small, Carla decided to join the Oklahoma Quilters' Guild

to work on her stitching. Now she's quilting like crazy, and her first bed-sized quilt, Midnight Starburst, won third place at the 1991 Oklahoma State Fair. It was also exhibited at the Inland Empire Quilter's Guild Quilt Show in Riverside, California, in 1992, and at A Celebration of Quilts Show in Oklahoma City in 1991.

Hunter's Star Variation by Marilyn Michael, Greenville, Pennsylvania. Marilyn made this quilt for a guild challenge, and it has since traveled the country and appeared in a number of shows since winning third place in *Miniature Quilt* magazine's Miniatures from the Heart contest in 1992. This delightful little quilt also took first place awards in Marilyn's guild's 1991 challenge and in the 1992 Penns Woods West Quilt Show in Mercer, Pennsylvania.

Starburst by Diane Doro, Des Moines, Iowa. Diane felt challenged when she heard other quilters talking about how they didn't like to use yellow in their quilts. She also wanted to make a quilt where the design of the quilt would "go beyond the boundaries of the individual blocks." She chose the Skyrocket pattern that originally appeared in *101 Patchwork Patterns* by Ruby McKim. Starburst received an honorable mention at the 1991 Iowa State Fair in the wallhanging division.

Blazing Star Table Runner by Cyndi Hershey, Lansdale, Pennsylvania. Owner of The Country Quilt Shop, in Chalfont, and quilt teacher, Cyndi designed this table runner using a traditional block first published in 1866 in *The Ladies' Friend.* Cyndi also has a background in interior design, which explains why choosing colors and fabrics and planning the design are her favorite parts of quiltmaking. Cyndi always likes to encourage her students to try new ideas and techniques, such as using lamé in projects as she did in this table runner.

Watermelon Wedges and **Sapphire's Window** by Mary Jane Cogan, Great Falls, Virginia. Mary Jane has a background in teaching and designing materials for an educational publisher but finds she is spending time now on more artistic endeavors, as a watercolor painter

and designer of needlework projects. She has had smocking patterns published in *The Smocking Arts,* but Watermelon Wedges and Sapphire's Window are Mary Jane's first published quilt designs. Mary Jane pieced and quilted Sapphire's Window specifically for this book, while her Watermelon Wedges design was machine pieced and quilted by Janet Coffman of Perkasie, Pennsylvania.

Christmas in July by Margie N. Bergan, McMinnville, Oregon. Margie reluctantly began quilting in 1982 at the urging of a friend to participate in making a raffle quilt. Since then quilts have become a big part of her life, as she is a member of three quilt guilds. Christmas in July is Margie's king-size adaptation of Ohio Christmas, a wall-hanging pattern by Gloria Parks, owner of Country Dry Goods in West Linn, Oregon, where Margie entered her quilt in the 1993 Labor of Love contest. Her quilt won at Country Dry Goods and was selected as a finalist in the same contest at the 1993 International Quilt Festival in Houston.

Christmas Rose by Mollie Fish, Corvallis, Oregon. Mollie is a quilter and designer who created this original Christmas wallhanging especially for *America's Best Quilting Projects.* She combined traditional red and green appliqué with pink highlights and a pieced checkerboard border in a pleasing design that looks wonderful at the holidays or anytime of the year.

Sawtooth Star Tree Skirt by Phyllis Dobbs, Birmingham, Alabama. Phyllis has been a needlework designer for the past nine years with her own company, Lucky Duck Designs. She has been working on quilt designs for the last four years. Christmas colors and projects are a favorite design theme for Phyllis, as evidenced by the Sawtooth Star Tree Skirt, which was created specifically for *America's Best Quilting Projects.*

Button Christmas Tree by Louy Danube, Merimac, Wisconsin. Louy is a graphic designer who branched out into designing craft projects and most recently began work on quilt designs. Her Button Christmas Tree features quick and easy techniques, plus a chance to use scraps of trims and left-over buttons in a creative way.

Introduction

To find this wonderful collection of quilts for *America's Best Quilting Projects,* we spent the past year traveling to quilt shows across the country. We saw quilts so beautiful they made us stop in our tracks and quilts so inspirational that we wanted to rush right home and start stitching. We were constantly amazed by the talent, creativity, and absolute love for quilting that just seems to grow stronger each year. We're pleased to be able to bring this collection of truly exceptional quilts and projects to you so you can enjoy them as much as we have.

You'll find a variety of bed quilts, wallhangings, even some smaller home decorating projects that represent the best in what quilters from Florida to Alaska have to offer. From time-honored traditional patterns—some with a new twist or two—to innovative uses of color and pattern, our hope is that as you page through this volume you'll find inspiration and renewed creativity. You may even find that you have a hard time deciding which project you want to make first!

This year we are happy to include a special section of star quilts. Stars have been a longtime favorite with quilters, and they are just as popular as ever, as evidenced by the seven delightful quilts you'll find in this book. Stars offer unending possibilities, and we think you'll be intrigued by the variety of uses stars play in the quilts we've selected.

In addition to showing you inspirational quilts, we also provide accurate step-by-step directions and easy-to-follow diagrams so you can stitch your own masterpieces. To help guide your project selection, each of the quilts in the book has a skill level rating of Easy, Intermediate, or Challenging. Our "Tips and Techniques" section provides all the basic quiltmaking information you need to complete any project in the book. Plus, you'll find additional technique boxes included with some of the projects themselves to guide you through methods for special touches that you may have never tried before, such as prairie points or piping. We've also sprinkled a variety of useful hints and tips throughout the book that can help you save time or trouble, so you'll want to keep an eye open for these!

We hope you enjoy your tour through *America's Best Quilting Projects.* It's been a truly delightful experience talking with each quilter, learning about her project, what inspired it, how long it took to complete, how often her husband had to make his own dinner or go without . . . well, you know what that's like. We'd like to thank each of the quilters who have been so generous in sharing their projects and ideas with us so we can in turn share them with you. To learn more about any of the projects and their makers, as well as shows where they've been exhibited and any awards they've won, take a look at the Acknowledgments section. Then get comfy, sit back, and enjoy the show.

Oh, and get out your shopping list. It's never too soon to start planning your next quilt!

Karen Soltys

Karen Costello Soltys
Project Editor

HEARTH
and
HOME

Gemstones

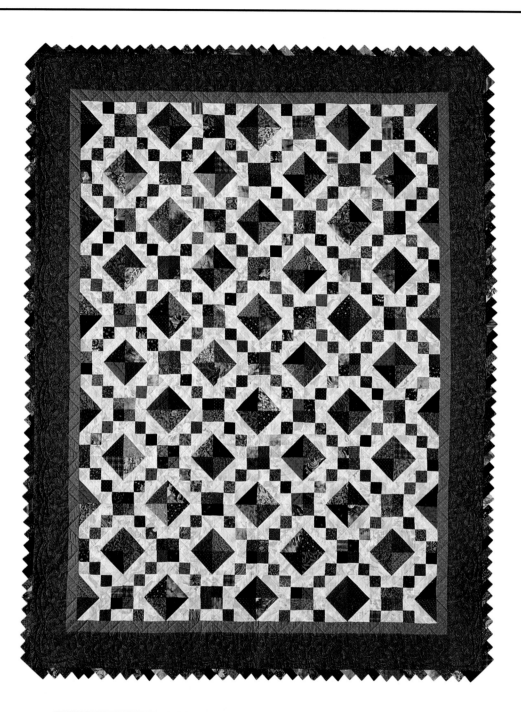

Quiltmaker: Jeanne Jenzano

Jeanne's prairie point edging works well on this quilt, playing off the many angles and diagonal lines within the design. To prove that looks can be deceiving, just one easy-to-piece block made of squares and triangles repeats to create this active and interesting pattern. Rich jewel-tone fabrics and a multifaceted design combine to create a dazzling quilt.

Skill Level: Easy

Size: Finished quilt is approximately 80 × 104 inches, not including the prairie point edging
Finished block is 8 inches square

Fabrics and Supplies

✓ 3½ yards of light print fabric for patch-work

✓ 3½ yards total of assorted medium and dark jewel-tone print fabrics for patch-work (You should have a minimum of ¼ yard per print.)

✓ ¾ yard of teal print fabric for inner border

✓ 2 yards of purple print fabric for outer border

✓ 3½ yards total of assorted medium and dark jewel-tone print fabrics for prairie point edging, *or* ¾ yard of fabric for binding

✓ 7½ yards of fabric for quilt back

✓ Queen-size quilt batting (90 × 108 inches)

✓ Rotary cutter, ruler, and mat

✓ Template plastic (optional)

Cutting

All measurements include ¼-inch seam allowances. The measurements for the borders include several extra inches in length; trim them to the exact length before sewing them to the quilt top. The instructions are written for quick-cutting the pieces using a rotary cutter and ruler. Cut all strips across the fabric. Note that for some of the pieces, the quick-cutting method will result in leftover strips of fabric.

You may want to cut just enough pieces to make one block to test your cutting and seam allowances for accuracy. If your finished block does not measure the size stated above, you can make adjustments before cutting all your fabric.

From the light print fabric, cut:
• 352 A squares
   Cut twenty-two 2½-inch strips for strip sets.

• 176 B triangles
   Cut eleven 4⅞-inch strips. From these strips cut 88 squares, each 4⅞ inches square. Cut each square in half diagonally to make two triangles.

From the medium and dark print fabrics, cut:
• 352 A squares
   Cut twenty-two 2½-inch strips for strip sets.

• 176 B triangles
   Cut eleven 4⅞-inch strips. From these strips cut 88 squares, each 4⅞ inches square. Cut each square in half diagonally to make two triangles.

From the teal print fabric, cut:
• Nine 2½-inch border strips

From the purple print fabric, cut:
• Nine 6½-inch border strips

From the fabrics for the prairie points, cut:
• One hundred eighty-two 5-inch squares
   Cut twenty-three 5-inch strips. From these strips cut 182 squares, each 5 inches square.

Fabric Key

☐ Light print

▨ Medium and dark prints

▨ Purple print

■ Teal print

Piecing the Blocks

1. Referring to the **Fabric Key** and **Strip Set Diagram,** make 22 strip sets by sewing together pairs of 2½-inch-wide light and dark strips. Press seam allowances toward the dark strips.

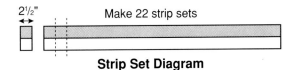

Strip Set Diagram

2. From the strip sets, cut 352 segments, each 2½ inches wide.

3. Join pairs of segments to form Four-Patch units as shown in **Diagram 1.** Press seam allowances to one side. Make 176 Four-Patch units.

4. Join a light B triangle to a dark B triangle along the long edges to form a Triangle-Square, as shown in **Diagram 2.** Press the seam allowance toward the dark triangle. Make 176 Triangle-Square units.

Make 176   Make 176

Four-Patch Unit   Triangle-Square
Diagram 1   **Diagram 2**

5. To piece one block, lay out two Triangle-Square units and two Four-Patch units as shown in the **Block Assembly Diagram.** Pay careful attention to the placement of light and dark fabrics within the block.

Make 80

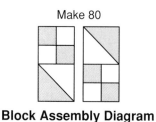

Block Assembly Diagram

6. Join units in two rows. Press seam allowances toward the Triangle-Square units. Join the rows. Press the seam allowance to one side. The block should measure 8½ inches square, including seam allowances.

7. Make 80 blocks. You will have extra Triangle-Squares and Four-Patch units to use for the top and bottom rows of the quilt top.

Assembling the Quilt Top

1. Referring to the **Quilt Diagram** and the photo on page 2, lay out the blocks in ten hori-zontal rows with eight blocks in each row. Note that the blocks are not all set in the same posi-tion. The positions alternate as shown in **Diagram 3.** Check to be sure all blocks are posi-tioned so the light-colored pieces create a sec-ondary design as shown. The heavy lines on the **Quilt Diagram** indicate the rows of blocks.

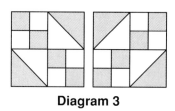

Diagram 3

2. Lay out the extra Triangle-Square and Four-Patch units to make a narrower row for the top and bottom edges of the quilt, as shown in **Diagram 4.** You will use eight Triangle-Squares and eight Four-Patch units for each row.

Top row

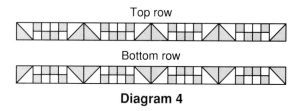

Bottom row

Diagram 4

3. Join the units in the top and bottom rows. Join the rest of the blocks in horizontal rows. Press the seam allowances in alternate directions from row to row.

4. Sew the rows together. Press the seam allowances to one side. The quilt top should measure 64½ × 88½ inches, including seam allowances.

5. For the top and bottom borders, join two teal border strips for each border. For the side borders, cut one teal border strip in half, then join two and one half border strips for each side border.

6. Measure the quilt from top to bottom through the center and trim the side borders to the correct length. Sew borders to the sides of the quilt top. Press the seam allowances toward the borders.

Quilt Diagram

7. Measure the width of the quilt, including the side borders, through the center. Trim the top and bottom borders to this measurement. Sew borders to the top and bottom ends of the quilt top. Press the seam allowances toward the borders.

8. Piece the outer borders from the purple print fabric and sew them to the quilt top in the same manner as you did for the inner border.

Quilting and Finishing

1. If you plan to finish the edges of your quilt with prairie points, prepare them and stitch them to the quilt top before layering and basting. See "Prairie Point Pizzazz" on the opposite page for details on making and attaching prairie points.

2. Mark desired quilting designs onto the quilt top. The quilting design used on the borders of the quilt shown is provided on this page.

If you are finishing the outer edges of the quilt with prairie points, leave at least ½ inch unquilted along the outer edge.

3. To piece the quilt back, divide the backing fabric into three 2½-yard pieces. Join the three panels; press the seam allowances toward the outer panels. The seams will run parallel to the top and bottom edges of the quilt.

4. Layer the quilt back, batting, and quilt top; baste. Trim the quilt back and batting so they are approximately 3 inches larger than the quilt top on all sides.

5. Quilt all marked designs, and add additional quilting as desired.

6. If you prefer to finish the quilt edges with binding, make approximately 380 inches of French-fold binding. See page 164 for suggested binding widths and instructions on making and attaching binding. Sew the binding to the quilt. Trim the excess batting and backing, and hand finish the binding on the wrong side of the quilt.

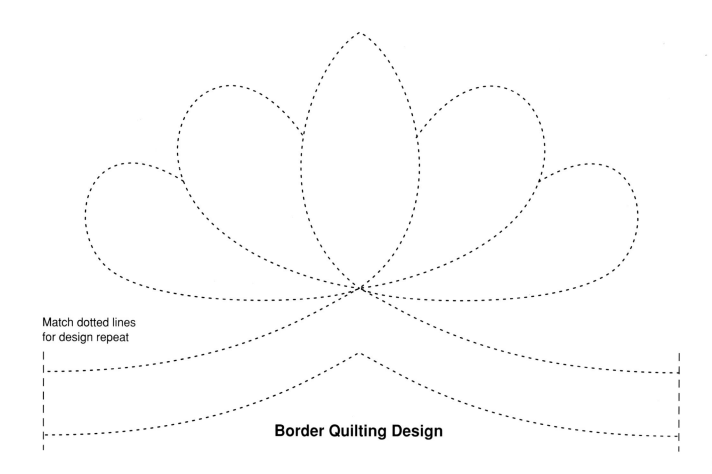

Match dotted lines for design repeat

Border Quilting Design

Prairie Point Pizzazz

1. For this quilt, you will need 182 squares, each 5 inches square. Fold each square in half diagonally with wrong sides together. Then fold it in half again, as shown in **Diagram 1,** to create the finished prairie point triangle.

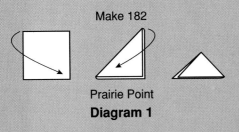

Make 182

Prairie Point

Diagram 1

2. To finish the edge of your quilt with prairie points, position the triangles so that the folds all face in the same direction. Slip the folded edge of each prairie point into the open edge of the prairie point next to it, as shown in **Diagram 2,** and pin or baste the prairie points to your quilt. The long edges of the triangles should be even with the raw edges of the quilt top. The quilt pictured has 37 prairie points on the top and bottom edges and 54 prairie points on each of the side

edges. You will need to adjust the spacing of prairie points on each side to make sure the points meet in the corners. Stitch the prairie points to the quilt top with a ¼-inch seam.

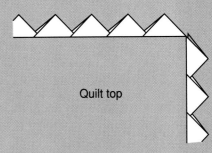

Quilt top

Diagram 2

3. After the quilting is finished, trim the backing and batting even with the edges of the quilt top. Then trim away an additional ¼ inch from the batting edges only to reduce bulk. Turn the triangles away from the quilt so the seam allowance is folded toward the wrong side of the quilt. Fold the backing and batting under a ¼ inch and pin them to the quilt so they cover the bottom edges of the prairie points. Blindstitch the backing in place to finish your quilt. ◆

Let It Grow

Quiltmaker: Sue Nickels

Appliqué flowers, sawtooth borders, lovely quilting designs, and a soft color palette complement one another in this cheery wall quilt. Inspired in part by an antique quilt, Sue designed Let It Grow as a project for her class on invisible machine appliqué and machine quilting. Not only her students love it; it received first prize for appliqué in her guild's yearly challenge. Although Sue used machine appliqué, you can work up this quilt using your favorite hand appliqué method.

Skill Level: Intermediate

Size: Finished quilt is 66 inches square
Finished appliqué block is 9 inches square

Fabrics and Supplies

- ✓ 1 yard of white print fabric for background squares and pieced border corner squares
- ✓ 1¾ yards of yellow print Fabric #1 for outer border, patchwork, and appliqué
- ✓ ¾ yard of yellow print Fabric #2 for sashing strips, patchwork, and appliqué
- ✓ ½ yard of yellow print Fabric #3 for outer border corner squares, sashing squares, patchwork, and appliqué
- ✓ ⅛ yard *each,* or scraps, of two or three additional yellow print and/or solid fabrics for patchwork and appliqué
- ✓ 1 yard of pink print fabric for middle border, patchwork, and appliqué
- ✓ ¼ yard of pink solid fabric for middle border corner squares, patchwork, and appliqué
- ✓ ¼ yard *total,* or scraps, of five or six additional pink print and/or solid fabrics for patchwork and appliqué
- ✓ ¾ yard of green print fabric for appliqué vine
- ✓ ¼ yard *total,* or scraps, of six to eight additional green print and/or solid fabrics for appliqué
- ✓ ½ yard of fabric for binding
- ✓ 4 yards of fabric for quilt back
- ✓ Twin-size quilt batting (72 × 90 inches)
- ✓ Rotary cutter, ruler, and mat
- ✓ Plastic-coated freezer paper or template plastic
- ✓ Tracing paper (optional)
- ✓ Black permanent marker
- ✓ 2 yards of 18-inch-wide lightweight fusible interfacing (optional)
- ✓ Fabric glue stick (optional)
- ✓ Clear nylon thread (optional)

Cutting

All measurements include a ¼-inch seam allowance. Measurements for the borders are longer than needed; trim them to the exact size when you add them to the quilt. Instructions given are for quick-cutting the background squares, sashing strips, border strips and squares, and the triangles for the sawtooth borders with a rotary cutter and ruler. Cut all strips across the fabric unless directed otherwise.

Patterns for appliqué pieces A through H begin on page 14. The patterns are finished size; add seam allowances when you cut the pieces from fabric. The quilt pictured was machine appliquéd. If you prefer to use hand appliqué, you may want to read through the tips on hand appliqué beginning on page 156 and choose the appliqué method you wish for the blocks. Either make plastic templates to mark and cut the appliqué pieces or make freezer paper templates.

Tip: *If you will be using machine appliqué, see "Five-Step Machine Appliqué" on page 11 for instructions on preparing templates, fusing fabric, and cutting pieces before you begin cutting your fabric.* ★

From the white print fabric, cut:
- Nine 9½-inch background squares
  Cut three 9½-inch strips. Cut the strips into 9½-inch squares.
- 8 J squares
  Cut one 1¾-inch strip. Cut the strip into 1¾-inch squares.

From the yellow print Fabric #1, cut:
- Four 8½ × 53-inch *lengthwise* outer border strips
- Reserve the remaining fabric to combine with other yellow fabrics to cut pieces for patchwork and appliqué

From the yellow print Fabric #2, cut:
- Twenty-four 1⅞ × 9½-inch sashing strips
  Cut six 1⅞-inch strips. Cut the strips into 9½-inch rectangles.
- Reserve the remaining fabric to combine with other yellow fabrics to cut pieces for patchwork and appliqué

From the yellow print Fabric #3, cut:

- Four 8½-inch outer border corner squares
  Cut one 8½-inch strip. Cut 8½-inch squares from the strip.

- 16 sashing squares
  Cut one 1⅞-inch strip. Cut 1⅞-inch squares from the strip.

- Reserve the remaining fabric to combine with other yellow fabrics to cut pieces for patchwork and appliqué

From the additional yellow print and/or solid fabrics and the remaining #1, #2, and #3 yellow print fabrics, cut:

- 256 I triangles
  Cut seven 2⅛-inch strips. Cut 128 squares, each 2⅛ inches square, from the strips. Cut each square diagonally into two triangles. Note: You will need to cut more than seven strips if your leftover fabric pieces are not 44 inches wide.

- 5 A tulip tips

- 5 G flower centers
  See "Crisp Appliqué Circles" on page 134 for a special circle technique.

From the pink print fabric, cut:

- Four 6¾-inch middle border strips

- Reserve the remaining fabric to combine with other pink fabrics to cut pieces for patchwork and appliqué

From the pink solid fabric, cut:

- Four 6¾-inch middle border corner squares
  Cut one 6¾-inch strip. Cut the strip into 6¾-inch squares.

- Reserve the remaining fabric to combine with other pink fabrics to cut pieces for patchwork and appliqué

From a variety of pink print and solid fabrics, cut:

- 256 I triangles
  Cut seven 2⅛-inch strips. Cut 128 squares, each 2⅛ inches square, from the strips. Cut each square diagonally into two triangles. Note: You will need to cut more than seven strips if your leftover fabric pieces are not 44 inches wide.

- 3 A tulip tips

- 8 C tulips

- 12 D hearts

- 5 F flowers

From the green print fabric, cut:

- Eight 1⅜ × 20-inch bias strips

From the additional green print and/or solid fabrics and the remaining green print fabric, cut:

- 88 E leaves

- 20 H leaves

- 4 B tulip stems

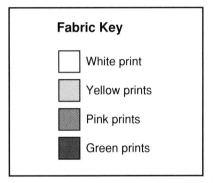

```
Fabric Key

☐  White print
▨  Yellow prints
▩  Pink prints
▦  Green prints
```

Making the Appliqué Blocks

1. Make master patterns for the rose and the tulip blocks to use as guides for positioning the appliqué pieces on the background squares. To make a master pattern, fold a 9-inch square of freezer or tracing paper in half vertically and horizontally for the rose block, and diagonally one way for the tulip block. Referring to the **Rose Block Diagram** and **Tulip Block Diagram**, trace around templates or patterns to make full-size drawings of the blocks. Darken the pattern outlines with the permanent marker.

Rose Block Diagram   **Tulip Block Diagram**

2. To make one block, begin by folding and lightly creasing a background square the same way you folded the paper for the master pattern for that block. Place the master pattern under the fabric square; pin the fabric square to the paper one.

3. Referring to the **Fabric Key,** prepare appliqué pieces for either hand or machine appliqué. Tips for hand appliqué are found on page 156. See "Five-Step Machine Appliqué" on this page for instructions on preparing your pieces for machine appliqué.

4. Use crease lines and the master pattern to help position the prepared appliqué pieces. Begin by positioning and pinning the appliqué pieces that are overlapped by others, pinning only through the fabric. Unpin the background square from the master pattern. Appliqué the pieces in place using thread that matches the appliqués. When making the Rose blocks, turn the blocks to the wrong side after appliquéing the F piece and trim away the background fabric, leaving a ¼-inch seam allowance, before adding G circles. See "Crisp Appliqué Circles" on page 134 for instructions on hand appliquéing perfect circles.

5. Make a total of five Rose blocks and four Tulip blocks.

Assembling the Quilt Center

1. Referring to the **Quilt Diagram,** lay out the nine completed blocks, the yellow sashing strips, and the sashing squares, making sure your Tulip blocks are placed in the right direction in the four corners.

2. Join the blocks, strips, and squares in horizontal rows. Four of the rows will have three sashing strips and four sashing squares. Three of the rows will have four sashing strips and three appliqué blocks. Press the seams toward the sashing strips. Join the rows to complete the inner quilt.

Piecing the Sawtooth Borders

1. Join a yellow and a pink I triangle to make a triangle-square, as shown in the diagram. Press seam allowances toward the pink fabrics. Make a total of 256 triangle-square units.

Make 256

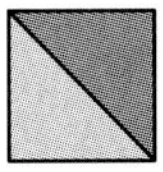

Triangle-Square

FIVE-STEP MACHINE APPLIQUÉ

1. Press a lightweight fusible interfacing to the wrong side of each of your appliqué fabrics.
2. For each shape in your appliqué design, cut a plastic template that includes the ¼-inch seam allowance. Trace around the plastic template on the interfacing side of your fabric and cut out.
3. For each piece that you are appliquéing, you will also need a freezer paper template. If you are making five tulips, cut five freezer paper tulips, *without* the seam allowance. Place the freezer paper template, shiny side up, on the wrong side (the interfacing side) of your appliqué piece. Press the seam allowances to the freezer paper to hold the raw edges in place. Do not press under seam allowances on edges that will be covered by overlapping pieces. Carefully remove the freezer paper after all edges have been pressed.
4. Position your appliqué pieces on the background fabric, using a glue stick or pins to hold them in place.
5. Using a blind stitch set at 20 stitches per inch, sew around the edges of your appliqué pieces. You should use clear nylon thread on the top and matching thread in the bobbin. Your stitches should catch the edge of your appliqué piece about every ¼ inch; see the diagram. Because the thread is invisible, this method is virtually indistinguishable from hand appliqué. ♦

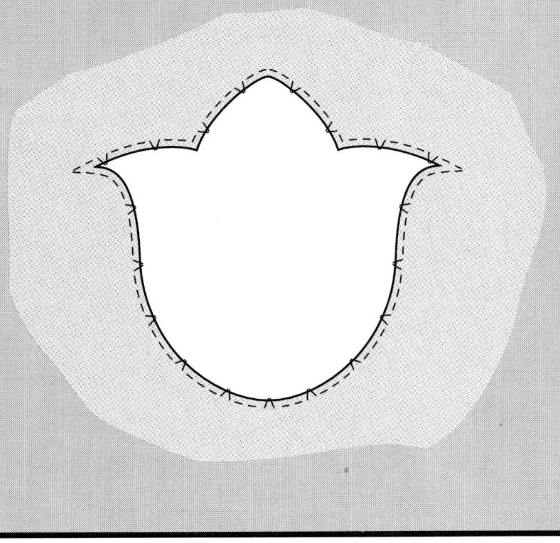

2. Join triangle-square units into long pieced border strips. For the inner pieced borders, make four sets of 26 triangle-squares, positioning the units as shown in the **Quilt Diagram.**

3. To make each outer pieced border, join 38 sets of triangle-squares, positioning the units as shown in the **Quilt Diagram.** Make four outer sawtooth borders.

Making the Appliqué Borders and Corner Squares

1. Referring to page 158 for instructions on preparing bias strips for appliqué, make eight 20-inch-long vines from the green strips. The finished width is approximately ½ inch.

2. Make master patterns for the border and the border corner. For the border pattern, cut a piece of freezer paper 6¾ × 35½ inches, or tape tracing paper together to make a piece this long. Make the corner pattern 8½ inches square. Fold and crease the border in half crosswise to find the center. Position the heart D template so the tip is touching the center crease. Trace the heart again on the other half of the crease, so the two heart points are touching. Position leaves so the inside tips are approximately 3 inches away from the starting point of the next leaf. Pairs of leaves should be approximately ½ inch apart to leave room for the vine. For the corner squares, position the tulip tip so it is approximately 2¼ inches from the block corner and the bottom of the tulip is approximately 3½ inches from the opposite block corner. Referring to the **Quilt Diagram,** trace around templates A, C, D, and E to make full-size border patterns. Darken pattern outlines.

3. To make one side border, begin by folding and lightly pressing one of the 6¾ × 35½-inch pink border strips in half both vertically and horizontally. Using the master pattern as a guide, position, pin, and appliqué the vine, leaves and hearts on the border strip. Stop stitching the vine approximately 1½ inches from the ends of the border. Let the excess vine hang loose; it will be stitched after the corner square has been added. Repeat to make a total of four side borders.

4. To make one corner square, fold a pink fabric square in half diagonally. Position, pin, and appliqué tulip tip and tulip in place. Leave the lower edge of the tulip unstitched so that the bias vine can be inserted later.

Attaching the Borders

1. Referring to the **Quilt Diagram** for directional placement, sew the inner sawtooth borders to the top and bottom of the quilt. Press seams toward the quilt center.

2. Sew a white J square to the ends of the remaining inner sawtooth borders. Press seams toward the squares. Sew the borders to the sides of the quilt. Press seams toward inner quilt.

3. Measure the quilt top, including seam allowances. Trim the pink appliqué borders to this measurement (approximately 35½ inches), trimming an equal amount from each end, and being careful not to cut excess bias vine. Sew borders to the top and bottom of the quilt top. Press the seams toward the appliqué borders.

4. Sew corner squares to the ends of the two remaining borders. Press seams toward the borders. Sew the borders to the sides of the quilt top. Press seams toward the appliqué borders.

5. Trim ends of the bias vine so they can be positioned under the lower edge of corner tulips. Appliqué the ends of the vines first, followed by the lower edge of the tulips.

6. Referring to the **Quilt Diagram,** sew the outer sawtooth borders to the top and bottom of the quilt. Press seams toward the quilt center.

7. Sew a white J square to the ends of the remaining outer sawtooth borders. Press seams toward squares. Sew the borders to the sides of the quilt. Press seams toward inner quilt.

8. Measure the quilt top, including seam allowances. Trim the four outer borders to this measurement which should be approximately 50½ inches. Sew the borders to the top and bottom of the quilt top. Press the seams toward the outer borders.

9. Sew the outer corner squares to the ends of the two remaining outer borders. Press seams toward the borders. Sew the borders to the sides of the quilt top. Press seams toward the outer borders.

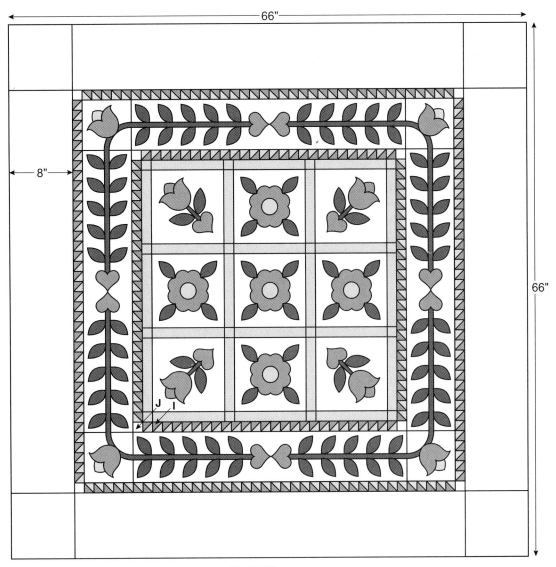

Quilt Diagram

Quilting and Finishing

1. Mark quilting designs. The design for the intersection of the sashing strips is on page 14. The quilt shown also has diagonal line quilting in the background of each flower block, outline quilting around all the appliqué pieces, and a wide feathered serpentine in the yellow border.

2. Cut the backing fabric into two equal lengths. Divide one piece in half lengthwise. Sew the two half panels to either side of the full panel along the long edges. Press seams in one direction.

3. Layer the quilt back, batting, and quilt top; baste. Trim the backing and batting so that they are 3 inches larger than the quilt top on all sides.

4. Quilt by hand or machine.

5. From the binding fabric, make approximately 275 inches of French-fold binding. See page 164 for suggested binding widths and instructions on making and attaching binding.

6. Sew the binding to the quilt top. Trim the excess batting and backing. Hand finish the binding on the wrong side of the quilt. See page 167 for instructions for adding a hanging sleeve.

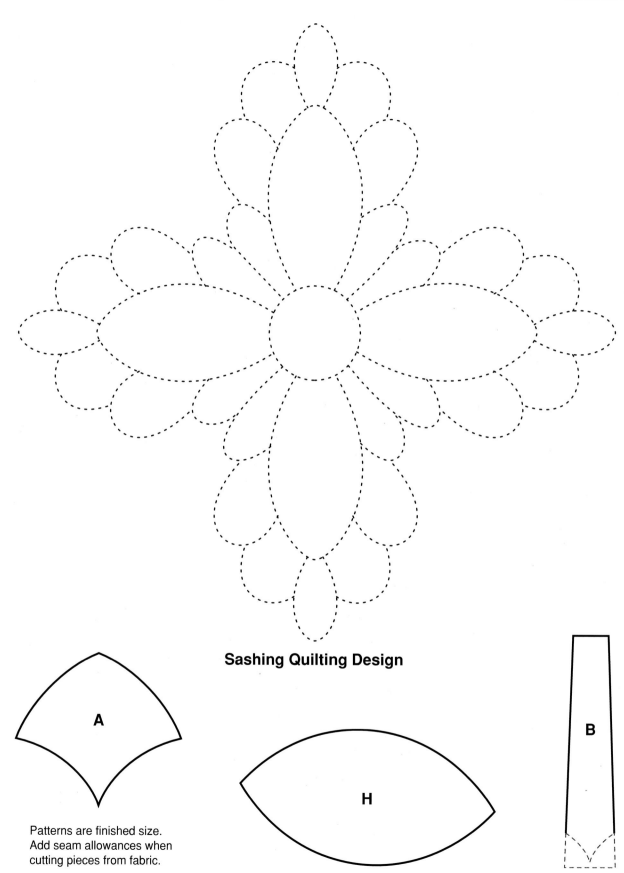

Sashing Quilting Design

A

Patterns are finished size.
Add seam allowances when
cutting pieces from fabric.

H

B

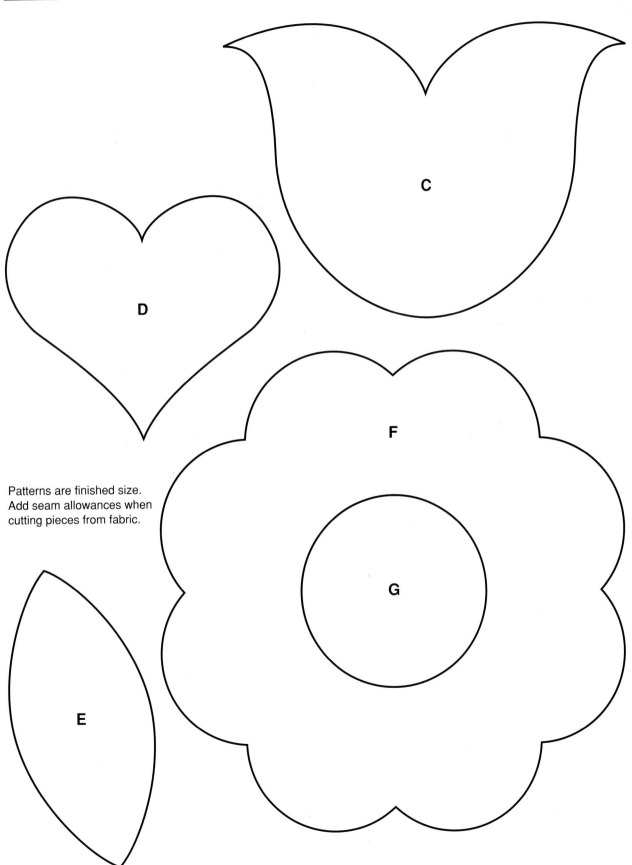

Patterns are finished size.
Add seam allowances when
cutting pieces from fabric.

Baskets of Love

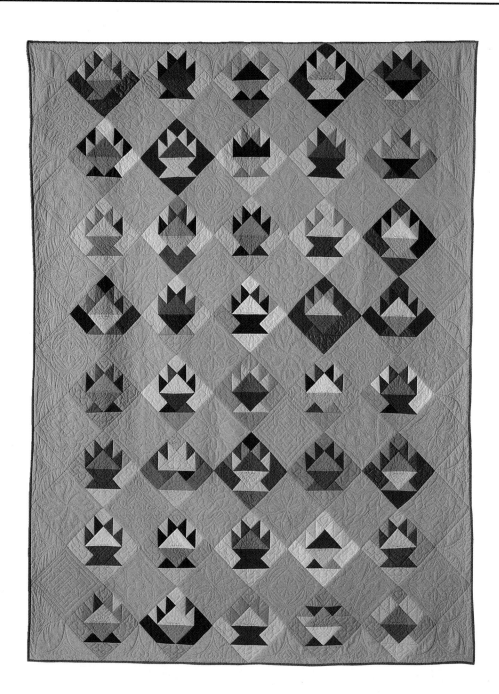

Quiltmaker: Connie Rodman

This quilt began as a wedding gift of 38 hand-pieced Cactus Basket blocks presented to Connie by her quilt club. She pieced two more blocks, then set them together using solid fabrics in desert colors that she felt fit the color theme of the quilt. Over 20 different hand-quilted designs add to the simple beauty of this quilt.

Skill Level: Easy

Size: Finished quilt is 84¾ × 113 inches
Finished block is 10 inches square (approximately 14⅛ inches on the diagonal)

Fabrics and Supplies

✓ 3½ yards of medium peach solid fabric for setting squares

✓ 2 yards of medium green solid fabric for setting triangles

✓ Fat quarters (18 × 22-inch rectangles), or the equivalent in scraps, of 20 to 25 different solid color fabrics for patchwork (Light, medium, and dark shades of colors such as blue, green, gold, pink, purple, rust, burgundy, and brown were used in the quilt shown.)

✓ ¾ yard of mauve solid fabric for binding

✓ 7⅞ yards of fabric for quilt back

✓ King-size quilt batting (120 inches square)

✓ Rotary cutter, ruler, and mat

✓ Template plastic (optional)

Cutting

All measurements include a ¼-inch seam allowance. The cutting instructions that follow give directions for quick-cutting the pieces with a rotary cutter and ruler. Cut all strips across the fabric width.

You may want to cut just enough pieces to make one block to test your cutting and seam allowances for accuracy. If your finished block does not measure the size stated above, you can make adjustments before cutting all your fabric.

From the medium peach solid fabric, cut:
• Forty-two 10½-inch setting squares
    Cut eleven 10½-inch strips. Cut the strips into 10½-inch squares.

From the medium green solid fabric, cut:
• 28 side setting triangles
    Cut four 15⅜-inch strips. Cut the strips into seven 15⅜-inch squares. Cut each square in half diagonally in both directions to make four triangles.

From the assorted solid color fabrics, cut a total of:
• 400 A triangles
    Cut thirty-four 3⅜-inch strips. From the strips, cut 200 squares, each 3⅜ inches square. Cut each square in half diagonally to make two triangles.

• 40 B squares
    Cut six 3-inch strips. Cut the strips into 3-inch squares.

• 120 C triangles
    Cut twenty 5⅞-inch strips. Cut the strips into 60 squares, each 5⅞ inches square. Cut each square in half diagonally to make two triangles.

• 80 D rectangles
    Cut twenty 3-inch strips. Cut the strips into 3 × 5½-inch rectangles.

Piecing the Blocks

For each block you will need ten A triangles, one B square, three C triangles, and two D rectangles. Choose the pieces randomly for each block so that no two blocks are the same; however, it's a good idea to make sure you have good contrast between parts of the block, such as the pairs of A triangles and the two C triangles that make up the center of the block.

1. Stitch four pairs of A triangles together along the long edges to make four triangle-square units as shown at the left in **Diagram 1.**

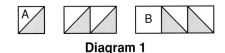
Diagram 1

2. Sew the triangle-squares together in pairs referring to **Diagram 1** for diagonal line placement. As shown, add a B square to the end of one of the triangle-square pairs, being sure to note the position of the diagonal lines. Press the seam toward the square.

3. Join two C triangles along their long edges to make a large triangle-square. Sew the pair of A triangle-squares to the C unit as shown in **Diagram 2.** Press the seam toward the C unit.

Diagram 2

4. Sew the triangle-squares with the attached B square to the side of the C unit as shown in **Diagram 3.**

Diagram 3

5. Sew the remaining two A triangles to the D rectangles as shown in **Diagram 4.** Sew these pieces to adjacent sides of the block as shown. Press the seams toward the side pieces.

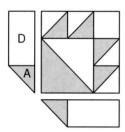

Diagram 4

6. Add a C triangle to complete the block as shown in **Diagram 5.** Press the seam toward the triangle. Repeat to make 40 basket blocks.

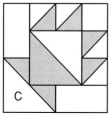

Diagram 5

Assembling the Quilt Top

1. Referring to the **Quilt Diagram,** lay out the blocks, setting squares, and side setting triangles in a pleasing color arrangement.

2. Join the blocks and setting pieces into diagonal rows. The heavy lines on the diagram indicate the rows. Press the seams toward the setting pieces.

3. Stitch the rows together, aligning the seam intersections.

Quilting and Finishing

1. Mark quilting designs. Among the quilting designs used on the quilt shown are a feathered heart motif in the center of the basket blocks and a triple heart design in the setting triangles. A variety of quilting designs were used in the plain setting squares. The two heart motifs and one of the quilting designs used in the setting squares are provided on pages 20–21. All seams are outline quilted.

2. Cut the backing fabric into three equal lengths and trim away selvages. Sew the three pieces together along the long edges. Press the seams away from the center panel. The seams will run parallel to the width of the quilt top.

3. Layer the quilt back, batting, and quilt top; baste. Trim the quilt back and batting so they are approximately 3 inches larger than the quilt top on all sides.

4. Quilt all marked designs.

5. From the binding fabric, make approximately 420 inches of French-fold binding. See page 164 for suggested binding widths and instructions on making and attaching binding.

6. Sew the binding to the quilt top. Trim the excess batting and backing, and hand finish the binding on the wrong side of the quilt.

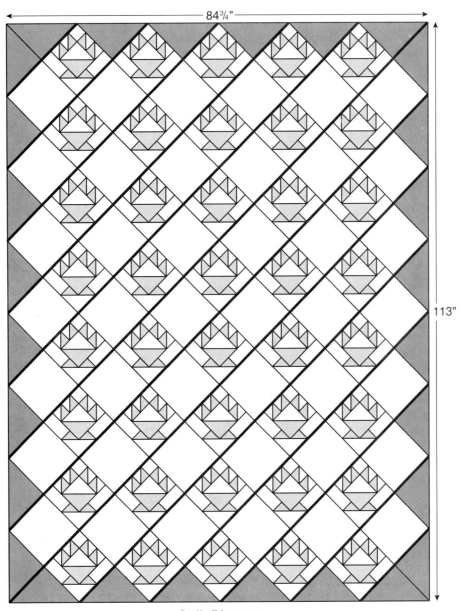

Quilt Diagram

Feathered Heart Quilting Design

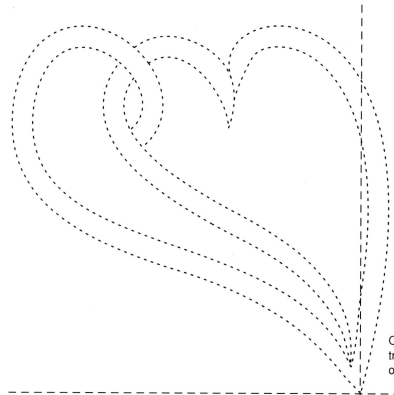

One-quarter of design; flip and
trace onto all four quarters
of template material

**Intertwined Heart Quilting Design
for Plain Squares**

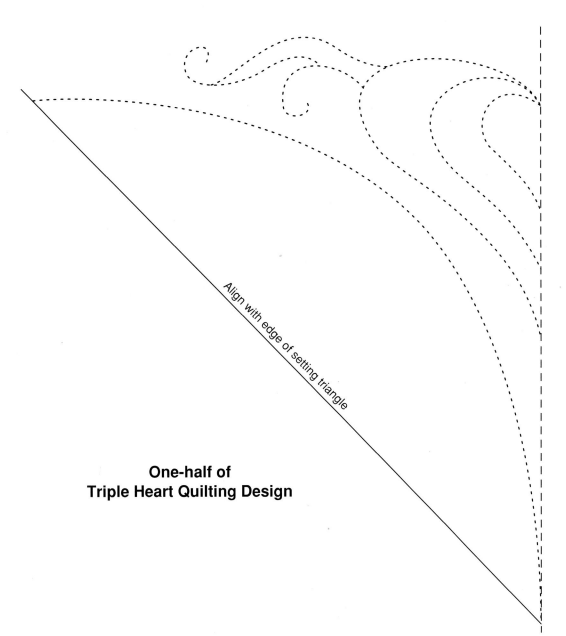

Align with edge of setting triangle

**One-half of
Triple Heart Quilting Design**

Overwhelmed by Autumn

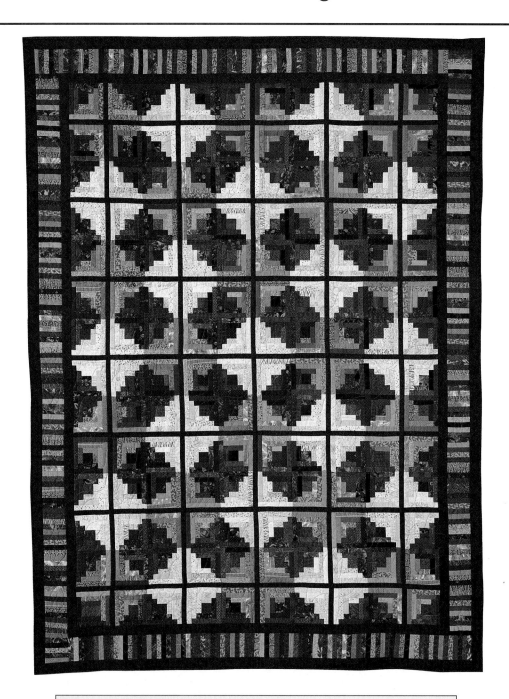

Quiltmaker: Diane Doro

Rich reds, browns, rusts, golds, and greens capture the essence of autumn as Diane saw it one lovely fall day as she and her husband were driving. Her new eyeglasses were bothering her too much to read, so she simply took them off and gazed out the window. Diane decided the fall colors were so beautiful when blurred together by her uncorrected vision that she just had to work them into a quilt! Diane machine quilted wavy lines across the Log Cabin blocks to represent leaves blowing in the wind.

Skill Level: Easy

Size: Finished quilt is approximately
69¾ × 92¼ inches
Finished Log Cabin unit is 5¼ inches square
Finished block is 10½ inches square

Fabrics and Supplies

- ✓ ¼ yard *each* of 14 assorted dark-value print fabrics, or scraps, to total 3½ yards for blocks and borders
- ✓ 3¼ yards of black with brown pindots fabric for borders, sashing, and binding
- ✓ ¼ yard *each* of 11 assorted medium-value print fabrics, or scraps, to total 2¾ yards for blocks and borders
- ✓ ¼ yard *each* of 7 assorted light-value print fabrics, or scraps, to total 1¾ yards for blocks
- ✓ 5½ yards of fabric for quilt back
- ✓ Full-size quilt batting (81 × 96 inches)
- ✓ Rotary cutter, ruler, and mat

Cutting

All measurements include ¼-inch seam allowances. The measurements for the borders include several extra inches in length; trim them to the exact length before sewing them to the quilt top. Instructions are given for quick-cutting all of the pieces using a rotary cutter and a ruler. Cut all strips across the fabric width unless directed otherwise. Note that for some of the pieces the quick-cutting method will result in left-over fabric.

You may want to cut just enough pieces to make one block to test your cutting and seam allowances for accuracy. If your finished block does not measure the size stated above, you can make adjustments before cutting all your fabric.

From the assorted dark fabrics, cut:
- 140 A squares
  Cut one 2-inch strip from *each* of seven different fabrics (seven strips total). From these strips, cut 140 squares, each 2 inches square.
- 140 *each* of pieces D, E, H, and I
  Cut fifty-five 1¼-inch strips. Refer to "Cutting Chart for Log Cabin Pieces" for lengths to cut the pieces from the strips.
- Twenty-four 1¼-inch strips for border strip sets

From the black with brown pindots fabric, cut a 99-inch-long piece. From this piece, cut:
- Eight 2 × 99-inch borders cut *lengthwise*
- Seven 1¼ × 58-inch sashing strips cut *lengthwise*
- Thirty 1¼-inch strips cut *crosswise*. From these strips cut:
  Thirty 11-inch sashing strips
  Ten 5¾-inch sashing strips
- Reserve the remaining fabric for binding

From the assorted medium fabrics, cut:
- 72 *each* of pieces B, C, F, G, J, and K
  Cut forty-five 1¼-inch strips. Refer to "Cutting Chart for Log Cabin Pieces" for lengths to cut the pieces from the strips.
- Twenty-four 1¼-inch strips for border strip sets

From the assorted light fabrics, cut:
- 68 *each* of pieces B, C, F, G, J, and K
  Cut forty-two 1¼-inch strips. Refer to "Cutting Chart for Log Cabin Pieces" for lengths to cut the pieces from the strips.

CUTTING CHART
FOR LOG CABIN PIECES

Begin with 1¼-inch strips. Cut assorted-length pieces from each fabric strip so that the fabric will be used in various locations in the blocks.

Piece	No. Cut from Fabric	Length of 1¼-inch Strip
B	72 medium, 68 light	2 inches
C	72 medium, 68 light	2¾ inches
D	140 dark	2¾ inches
E	140 dark	3½ inches
F	72 medium, 68 light	3½ inches
G	72 medium, 68 light	4¼ inches
H	140 dark	4¼ inches
I	140 dark	5 inches
J	72 medium, 68 light	5 inches
K	72 medium, 68 light	5¾ inches

Piecing the Log Cabin Units

You will need to make 140 Log Cabin units for the quilt. Sixty-eight of these use light-value fabrics for the light half of the unit. Seventy-two of the units use medium-value fabrics for the light half. The most efficient way to piece the units is to do the same step for all units of one type in assembly-line fashion. Take accurate ¼-inch seams when sewing. Press seam allowances away from the center square.

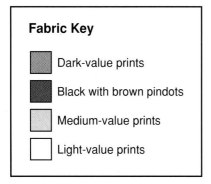

Fabric Key

- Dark-value prints
- Black with brown pindots
- Medium-value prints
- Light-value prints

1. Referring to the **Fabric Key,** begin by sewing a B strip to an A center square, as shown in **Diagram 1.** (The diagram shows light fabrics being used; remember that you need to make blocks with medium fabrics as well.)

Diagram 1

2. Sew a C strip to the long side of the Step 1 unit, as shown in **Diagram 2.**

Diagram 2

3. Referring to **Diagram 3,** continue to add lettered strips in order around the center until all eight strips have been added, forming a Log

Cabin unit. The completed units should measure 5¾ inches, including seam allowances. Repeat until you have 68 units made with light fabrics and 72 made with medium fabrics in the light portion of the unit.

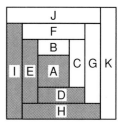

Diagram 3

Making the Full Blocks

1. Use two Log Cabin units with light fabrics and two units with medium fabrics to make each block. Lay out units as shown in the **Log Cabin Block Diagram,** paying careful attention to placement of light, medium, and dark areas.

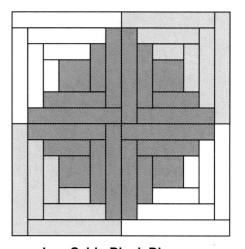

Log Cabin Block Diagram

2. Sew units together in two rows with two units in each row. Press seam allowances toward the blocks with light fabrics. Join the rows. Press seam allowance to one side. Repeat to make 24 blocks.

Making the Half-Blocks

1. Choose one Log Cabin unit with light fabrics and one unit with medium fabrics for each half-block.

2. Make ten half-blocks as in **Diagram 4A** and ten as in **Diagram 4B** by joining pairs of blocks. Press seam allowances to one side. You will have four Log Cabin units with medium fabrics left to use at the corners of the quilt top.

A

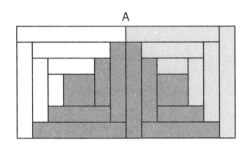

B

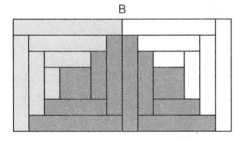

Diagram 4

Assembling the Inner Quilt Top

1. Referring to the **Quilt Diagram** and the photo on page 22, lay out the blocks, half-blocks, corner blocks, and sashing pieces in eight horizontal rows. Pay careful attention to the placement of the light and medium areas.

2. For the top and bottom rows, join corner blocks and half-blocks with short sashing strips between them. Press seam allowances toward the sashing strips.

3. To make the full-block rows, join half-blocks and blocks with sashing strips between them. Press seam allowances toward the sashing strips.

4. Measure the length of a row. Trim the long sashing strips to this length (approximately 56¾ inches).

5. Join the rows and sashing strips. Press seam allowances toward the sashing strips.

Making the Pieced Borders

1. Choose three dark strips and three medium strips for a strip set. Referring to **Diagram 5,** sew the six strips together, alternating medium and dark strips. Press seam allowances to one side. Make eight different strip sets.

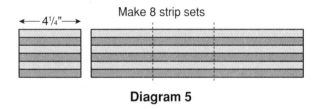

Make 8 strip sets

←—4¼"—→

Diagram 5

2. Cut a total of sixty-six 4¼-inch segments from the strip sets.

3. To make each side border, join 19 segments. Press seam allowances to one side.

4. To make the top and bottom border, join 14 segments for each border. Press seam allowances to one side.

Adding the Borders

1. Measure the length of the quilt top through the center. Trim two black borders to this length (approximately 79¼ inches). Sew borders to the sides of the quilt top. Press seam allowances toward the borders.

2. Measure the width of the quilt top through the center, including the side borders. Trim two black borders to this length (approximately 59¾ inches). Sew borders to the top and bottom edges of the quilt top. Press seam allowances toward the borders.

3. Pin a pieced border to the bottom edge of the quilt top. Leave five fabric strips extending beyond one edge of the black border. Sew the border to the quilt top, leaving approximately 6

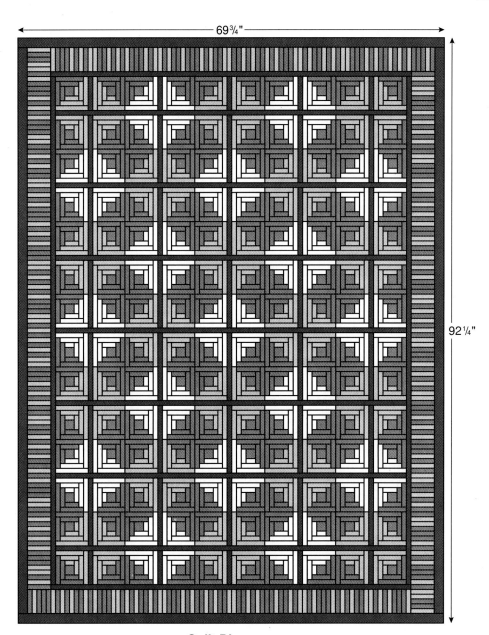

Quilt Diagram

inches unsewn at the end that extends beyond the black border **(Diagram 6A).** This seam will be finished after the other borders have been added. Press seam toward the black border.

4. See **Diagram 6B** for the order of adding borders. Pin a pieced border to the right side of the quilt top. Position the border so it will be sewn to the short end of the bottom border. The opposite end of the side border should be even with the top edge of the top black border. Sew the border to the quilt, sewing the complete seam. Press seam allowance toward the black border.

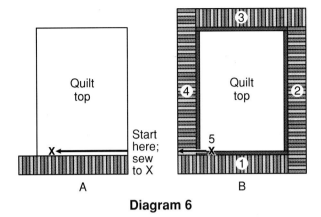

Diagram 6

Quilting and Finishing

1. Mark quilting designs if desired. The quilt shown is machine quilted in the ditch along all sashing seams and along the black border edges. The Log Cabin blocks are also randomly quilted with wavy lines.

2. Divide the backing fabric into two 2¾-yard pieces. Divide one panel in half lengthwise. Sew a half panel to each long side of the full panel. Press the seam allowances away from the center panel.

3. Layer the quilt back, batting, and quilt top; baste. Trim the quilt back and batting so they are approximately 3 inches larger than the quilt top on all sides.

4. Hand or machine quilt as desired.

5. From the black fabric, make approximately 350 inches of French-fold binding. See page 164 for suggested binding widths and instructions on making and attaching binding.

6. Sew the binding to the quilt. Trim excess batting and backing, and hand finish the binding to the wrong side of the quilt.

5. In a similar manner, sew a pieced border to the top edge of the quilt and then to the left side, as shown in **Diagram 6B.**

6. Complete the seam on the bottom pieced border, sewing along the short end of the left side border.

7. Following the instructions in Steps 1 and 2, trim and sew black borders to the sides and then the top and bottom edges of the quilt top. Press seam allowances toward the black borders.

Great-Grandma Goebel's Bridal Quilt

Quiltmaker: Elsie Campbell

This stunning appliqué quilt was inspired by one made in 1857 by Elsie's grandmother when she was just 18. The original quilt had cross-hatching rather than echo quilting on the blocks, and corner turns Elsie described as "unique, but not very accurate." In her adaptation, Elsie drafted her own border feather designs for a perfect fit and boldly quilted them in red! An extra and unexpected touch of red piping creates a handsome frame for the quilted borders.

Skill Level: Challenging

Size: Finished quilt is 84 inches square
Finished block is 20 inches square

Fabrics and Supplies

- ✓ 6¾ yards of white solid fabric for outer border, appliqué blocks, sawtooth border, and binding
- ✓ 2 yards of red solid fabric for edge piping, sawtooth border, and appliqué pieces
- ✓ 2 yards of green solid fabric for appliqué pieces
- ✓ 2½ yards of 90-inch-wide fabric for quilt back
- ✓ Queen-size quilt batting (90 × 108 inches)
- ✓ Rotary cutter, ruler, and mat
- ✓ Plastic-coated freezer paper and/or template plastic
- ✓ Tracing paper
- ✓ Black permanent marker
- ✓ 9¼ yards of ⅛-inch-diameter cotton cording
- ✓ Zipper foot or cording foot for sewing machine

Cutting

All measurements include a ¼-inch seam allowance. The instructions are written for quick-cutting background squares, border strips, and patchwork pieces with a rotary cutter and ruler. Measurements for the outer borders are longer than the quilt dimensions. Do not trim off the extra fabric; it will be used to miter the border corners.

Patterns for the appliqué pieces A, B, C, and D are provided on pages 32 and 34. When making A, B, and C templates, cut out inner areas as indicated for reverse appliqué. The cutting instructions include both B and B reverse. See "Working with Reverse Appliqué Templates" on page 30 for directions on cutting reverse pieces for appliqué. Appliqué patterns are finished size; add seam allowances when you cut the pieces from the fab-

ric. Read through the tips under "Hand Appliqué" beginning on page 156 and choose the appliqué method you wish to use for making the blocks.

You may want to cut just enough pieces to make one block to test your cutting and seam allowances for accuracy.

From the white solid fabric, cut two 2½-yard lengths. From each length, cut:
- Two 9½ × 90-inch borders
- Four 22-inch squares

From the remaining white solid fabric, cut:
- One 22-inch square
- 172 border triangles
  Cut five 2⅜-inch crosswise strips. Cut the strips into 86 squares, each 2⅜ inches square. Cut each square diagonally into two triangles.
- Reserve the remaining fabric for binding

From the red solid fabric, cut:
- One 20-inch square for making continuous bias strips for piping
- 172 border triangles
  Cut five 2⅜-inch crosswise strips. Cut the strips into 86 squares, each 2⅜ inches square. Cut each square diagonally into two triangles.
- 9 A appliqué pieces (Trace around the edge of the cutout center flower shape to form a fold-under line for reverse appliqué. *Do not* cut out the interior shape yet.)
- 72 insert strips for B appliqués
  Cut two 2½-inch crosswise strips. Cut the strips into 72 segments, each 1 × 2½ inches.
- 36 insert strips for C appliqués
  Cut one 2½-inch crosswise strip. Cut the strip into 36 segments, each ¾ × 2½ inches.
- 36 D appliqué pieces

From the green solid fabric, cut:
- Nine 3-inch circles
- 36 B and 36 B reverse appliqué pieces (Trace along the edge of the cutout teardrop shape to form a fold-under line for reverse appliqué. *Do not* cut out the interior shape yet.)
- 36 C appliqué pieces (Mark cutout shapes as described for B pieces.)

Appliquéing the Blocks

1. Make a master pattern for the appliqué design to use as a guide for positioning the appliqué pieces on the background squares. Fold a large sheet of tracing paper in half both ways. Refer to the **Block Diagram,** and trace around templates or patterns to make a full-size drawing of the block. Darken the pattern outlines with a permanent marker.

Block Diagram

2. To make one block, fold a white fabric square in half vertically, horizontally, and diagonally in both directions. Crease lightly. Center the master appliqué pattern under the fabric square; pin the fabric square to the paper square.

3. Use crease lines and the master pattern to help position an A appliqué piece at the center of the background square; pin the appliqué in place, pinning only through the two fabrics. Unpin the background square from the master pattern. Appliqué the A piece in place.

4. Cut out the central shape, cutting a scant ¼ inch to the *inside* of the marked lines to allow for turn under, and being careful not to cut into the background square. Position a 3-inch green circle in the cut opening. Hold the square up to a window or use a light table to help position the insert

symmetrically. Pin the green piece in place. Turn under the edges of the opening and appliqué.

5. Use the master pattern and crease lines to position and appliqué the B appliqués one at a time on the background square. After appliquéing, cut out the teardrop shape as described above for the A appliqué. Slip a red insert into the opening. Turn under opening edges and appliqué.

6. Use the master pattern and crease lines to position and pin a red D piece in place. Position a red C insert strip so it will lie under the C appliqué piece. Position and pin a C appliqué piece in place. When all three pieces have been positioned correctly, appliqué D first, then C. Cut lengthwise slits in the reverse appliqué openings, then turn edges under and appliqué.

7. Use a large plastic ruled square or ruler and trim each block to 20½ inches square. Repeat to make a total of nine blocks.

WORKING WITH REVERSE APPLIQUÉ TEMPLATES

The easiest way to make reverse appliqué pieces is with plastic templates. Using the patterns on pages 32 and 34, make plastic templates for A, B, and C appliqués. Cut out the reverse appliqué areas on each template. Make a cut from an outside edge into the middle area in order to cut out small inner motifs, then mend the cut with a piece of masking tape. Use the hard-edged templates to mark your fabric pieces. Add a scant ¼-inch seam allowance when you cut your fabric pieces. Ignore the inner reverse appliqué shapes at this point. Appliqué the shapes in place, using your preferred hand appliqué method. Place the plastic template atop the completed appliqué. Mark along the edges of openings for reverse appliqué. Cut out the openings leaving a scant ¼-inch *inside* of the marked edge, and being careful not to cut into background fabric. Slide contrasting fabric into the opening, turn raw edges of the opening under, and appliqué to the contrasting fabric. ◆

Piecing the Sawtooth Border

1. Join white and red triangles to make a total of 172 triangle-square units as shown. Press seams toward the red triangles.

Make 172

2. Join 42 triangle-square units as shown in the **Quilt Diagram** to make one border strip. Repeat to make three more strips. The remaining four triangle-squares will be used for border corners.

Assembling the Quilt Top

1. Lay out the nine appliqué blocks in three rows of three blocks per row. Join the blocks into three rows. Press seam allowances in opposite directions from row to row. Join the rows matching block intersections.

2. As shown in the **Quilt Diagram,** sew a sawtooth border strip to two opposite sides of the quilt top. Press seam allowances toward the quilt top.

Tip: If the sawtooth border does not fit your quilt top, make small adjustments in many of the seams, rather than larger adjustments in just a few of the seams, so your adjustments will be unnoticeable. ★

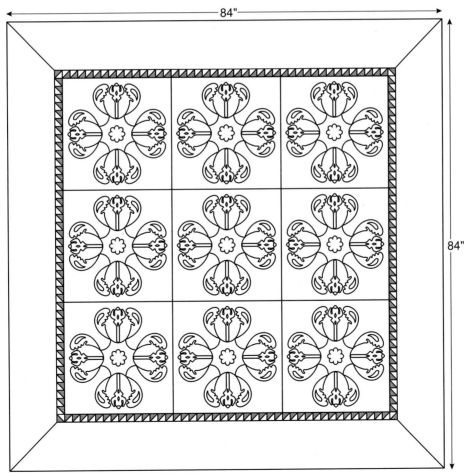

Quilt Diagram

3. Referring to the **Quilt Diagram** for directional placement of seams, sew triangle-squares to the opposite ends of the two remaining border strips. Press seam allowances toward the corner units. Sew the border strips to the remaining sides of the quilt top. Press seam allowances toward the quilt top.

4. Sew the white outer borders to the quilt top. Your border strips will be longer than your quilt length. *Do not cut off excess fabric.* The extra length will be needed to miter the corners of the borders. Press the seam allowances toward the borders. Miter the border corner seams, referring to page 160 for more detailed directions.

Quilting and Finishing

1. Mark quilting designs on the quilt top. Designs for the A appliqué pieces are printed on the pattern piece on page 34. The quilt shown has echo quilting on the blocks and a triple line of quilting between the border plumes. The quiltmaker used white quilting thread for the echo quilting and red thread to make her fancy designs stand out.

2. Layer the quilt back, batting, and quilt top; baste. Trim the quilt back and batting so they are approximately 3 inches larger than the quilt top on all sides.

3. Quilt all marked designs, and add additional quilting as desired, such as echo quilting.

4. If you will be adding edge piping as for the quilt shown, first baste the layers of the quilt together a scant ¼ inch from the raw edges of the quilt top. Then follow the directions in "Perfect Piping" on the opposite page.

5. Before cutting binding strips, experiment with binding width. You will need to cut binding wider than usual to accommodate the raw edges of the piping fabric. From the white fabric, make approximately 360 inches of French-fold binding. See page 164 for instructions on making binding.

6. Sew the binding to the quilt top using a zipper foot. Before turning and hand finishing the binding, check to see that you covered the cording stitches when you sewed on the binding. Re-stitch sections as needed. Trim the excess batting and backing, and hand finish the binding on the wrong side of the quilt.

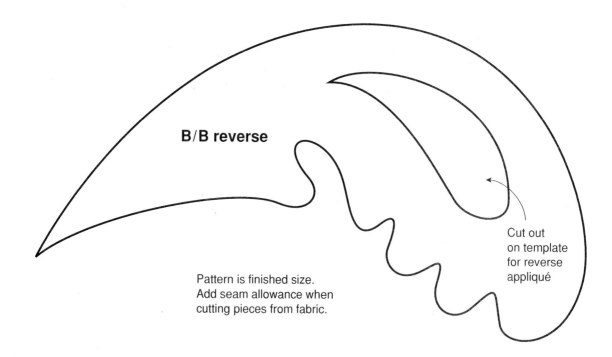

B/B reverse

Pattern is finished size.
Add seam allowance when
cutting pieces from fabric.

Cut out
on template
for reverse
appliqué

PERFECT PIPING

1. To make the piping, make continuous binding, following instructions on page 164. Use a 20-inch square of red solid fabric and cut the binding 1¼ inches wide. Fold the long red bias strip in half, wrong sides together, and insert the cording. Using a zipper foot and a basting stitch, sew the cording into the strip, leaving space between the cording and the row of stitching so you will have room for stitching the cording to the quilt.

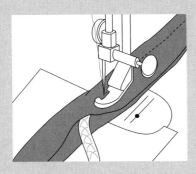

2. Baste the cording to the quilt before adding binding. Lay the corded strip on the quilt top, aligning raw edges with those of the quilt. Stitch the cording to the quilt top, using the zipper foot and a machine basting stitch. Begin stitching along one side of the quilt, not at a corner. Leave approximately 2 inches unstitched at the beginning point. Stop stitching 1 inch before the corner. To turn the corner sharply, clip the seam allowance of the cording several times near the corner, clipping not quite to the stitching line. Continue stitching into the corner. Stop stitching exactly at the corner and leave the needle down. Lift the presser foot and pivot the quilt 45 degrees. Take two stitches, stopping with the needle down again. Lift the presser foot and pivot, positioning the quilt to stitch the next straight side. Align the raw edges of the piping with the quilt and continue stitching until you approach your starting point.

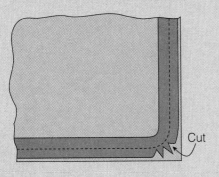
Cut

3. As you near the starting point, cut the cording so that you will have approximately 1 inch to overlap where you started.

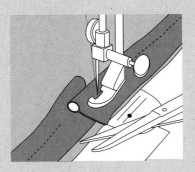

4. Open stitches on the ending piece and trim cording (not the extra fabric) so it will exactly abut the beginning end of the cording.

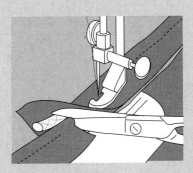

5. Fold under ¼ inch of the fabric strip on the ending piece. Insert the beginning piece into the ending piece, aligning raw edges of fabric. Continue stitching across the joining section. ◆

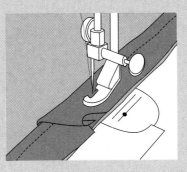

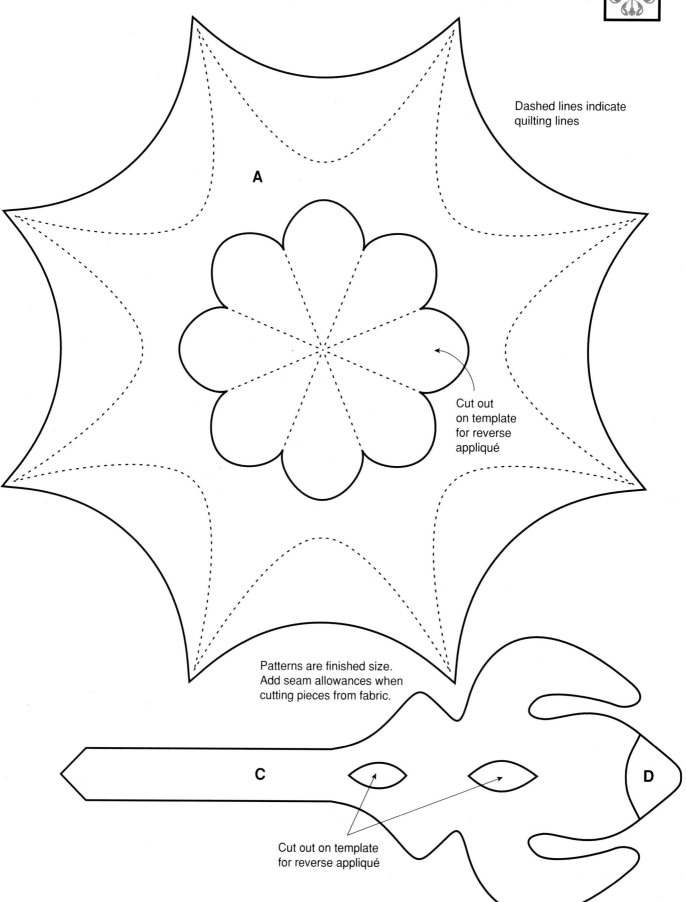

Dashed lines indicate
quilting lines

A

Cut out
on template
for reverse
appliqué

Patterns are finished size.
Add seam allowances when
cutting pieces from fabric.

C

D

Cut out on template
for reverse appliqué

Bringing Lilies to the Table

Quiltmaker: Adrienne-Joy Chiet

Adrienne-Joy designed this quilt as a game table topper so her family could enjoy her beautiful quilting while they played. Four Lily Basket blocks arranged in a garden maze setting grace the table top, while a border of appliquéd lilies, diamond-shaped leaves, and a gently curving vine sweeps around the quilt center and gently frames it.

Skill Level: Intermediate

Size: Finished quilt is 55 inches square
Finished block is 14 inches square

Fabrics and Supplies

- ✓ 2¼ yards of muslin for borders, patchwork, and sashing strips
- ✓ 1⅓ yards of dark green paisley stripe fabric with at least four repeats of a given stripe across the fabric width for borders
- ✓ 1 yard of dark green solid fabric for patchwork, stems, vine, and border appliqué
- ✓ ¾ yard of burgundy paisley fabric for sashing
- ✓ ¾ yard of burgundy solid fabric for patchwork and binding
- ✓ ⅓ yard of medium rose solid fabric for patchwork
- ✓ ¼ yard of dark green paisley fabric for baskets
- ✓ ⅛ yard, or scraps, of medium green solid fabric for border appliqué
- ✓ 3½ yards of fabric for quilt back
- ✓ Twin-size quilt batting (72 × 90 inches)
- ✓ Rotary cutter, ruler, and mat
- ✓ Template plastic
- ✓ ¼-inch-wide Celtic or bias bar (optional)

Cutting

All measurements include ¼-inch seam allowances. Measurements for the outer borders are longer than the quilt dimensions. Do not trim off the extra fabric; it will be used to miter the border corners. The instructions are written for quick-cutting the borders, sashing pieces, and the B, C, D, E, G, H, I, and J pieces for the blocks using a rotary cutter and a ruler. Cut all strips across the fabric width unless directed otherwise. Note that for some of the pieces, the quick-cutting method will result in leftover strips of fabric. Make templates for pattern pieces A, F, X, and

Y on pages 40–41. Instructions for making and using templates are on page 153. If you prefer to cut all pieces in a traditional manner, make templates for pieces B, C, D, E, G, H, I, and J using the dimensions given in the cutting directions.

Because the flower portions of the Lily Basket blocks require precision piecing and setting in the C and D pieces, refer to "Setting-In Pieces" on page 155 for tips on marking set-in pieces. You may want to cut just enough pieces to make one block to test your templates, cutting, and seam allowances for accuracy. If your finished block does not measure the size stated above, you can make adjustments before cutting all your fabric.

From the muslin, cut one 57-inch-long piece. From this piece, cut:

- Four 6½ × 57-inch *lengthwise* borders

- 4 J triangles
  Cut two 5½-inch squares. Cut each square in half diagonally to make two triangles.

- 8 E triangles
  Cut one 5¾ × 25-inch strip. Cut the strip into four 5¾-inch squares. Cut each square in half diagonally to make two triangles.

- 4 F rectangles
  Use Template F
  OR
  Cut one 4½ × 25-inch strip. Cut the strip into four 4½ × 5⅜-inch rectangles.

- 12 D squares
  Cut two 2½ × 25-inch strips. Cut the strips into twelve 2½-inch squares.

- 24 C triangles
  Cut one 2⅞ × 40-inch strip. Cut the strip into twelve 2⅞-inch squares. Cut each square in half diagonally to make two triangles.

From the remaining muslin, cut:

- Four 4½ × 18½-inch sashing strips
  Cut two 4½-inch strips. Cut the strips into four 4½ × 18½-inch rectangles.

- 8 H rectangles
  Cut two 2¾-inch strips. Cut the strips into eight 2¾ × 10-inch rectangles.

From the dark green paisley stripe fabric, cut:

- Four 2 × 47-inch *lengthwise* borders cut from identical repeats of the stripe

From the dark green solid fabric, cut:
- 16 B triangles
  Cut one 3¾-inch strip. Cut the strip into eight 3¾-inch squares. Cut each square in half diagonally to make two triangles.
- 24 Y diamonds
- Reserve the remaining fabric for ¾-inch continuous bias for stems and vine

From the burgundy paisley fabric, cut:
- Eight 2½ × 14½-inch sashing strips
  Cut four 2½-inch strips. From the strips cut eight 2½ × 14½-inch rectangles.
- Eight 2½ × 18½-inch sashing strips
  Cut four 2½-inch strips. From the strips cut eight 2½ × 18½-inch rectangles.
- Sixteen 2½-inch squares to form triangles on the ends of muslin sashing strips
  Cut one 2½-inch strip. From the strip cut 16 squares, each 2½ inches square.
- One 4½-inch sashing center square

From the burgundy solid fabric, cut:
- 32 A diamonds
- Reserve the remaining fabric for binding

From the medium rose solid fabric, cut:
- 32 A diamonds

From the dark green paisley fabric, cut:
- 4 G triangles
  Cut two 7¾-inch squares. Cut each square in half diagonally to make two triangles.
- 8 I triangles
  Cut four 3⅛-inch squares. Cut each square in half diagonally to make two triangles.

From the medium green solid fabric, cut:
- 4 X diamonds

Piecing the Lily Units

1. Referring to the **Fabric Key** and **Diagram 1,** lay out two rose A diamonds and two burgundy A diamonds to form half a star, placing the rose diamonds together in the center. Sew two diamonds together to form a pair; join two pairs to form the lily. Stitch only from matching point to matching point. Backstitch at the beginning and end of seams without stitching into the seam allowances.

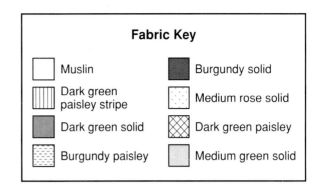

2. Sew a dark green solid B triangle to the lower edge of each half star, as shown in **Diagram 2.**

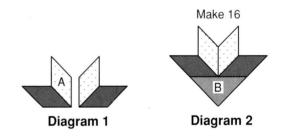

Diagram 1   **Diagram 2**

3. Repeat to make a total of 16 lily units.

4. Baste under the seam allowances around four of the lily units to prepare them for the appliquéd border. Set border lily units aside.

Preparing the Bias for Stems and Vine

1. Cut approximately 280 inches of ¾-inch continuous bias for your stems and vine. Refer to "Making Bias Strips for Stems and Vines" on page 158 for instructions on making bias strips.

2. Cut 12 stems, each 6 inches long, from the prepared bias. Reserve the remaining bias for the border vine.

3. Using the placement guides on pattern F, appliqué stems to the F rectangles.

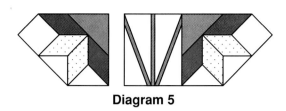

Diagram 5

Piecing the Blocks

1. Lay out three lily units and the remaining pieces needed for one Lily Basket block, as shown in **Diagram 3.** As you assemble the blocks, press seam allowances toward darker fabrics when possible.

Make 4

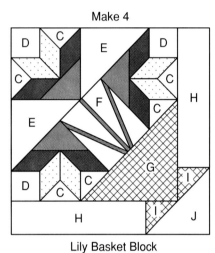

Lily Basket Block

Diagram 3

2. Set C triangles and D squares into openings on lily units. See page 155 for tips on setting in pieces.

3. Sew E triangles to the lower sides of the top lily, as shown in **Diagram 4.**

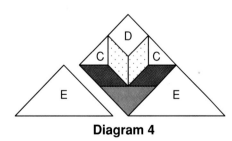

Diagram 4

4. Sew a side lily to opposite sides of the F piece so the points of the B triangles match up with the appliquéd stems. See **Diagram 5.** Sew this unit to the top lily section.

5. Sew a G basket triangle to the lower edge of the bottom lily section, forming a square.

6. Sew an I basket base triangle to one short end of both H rectangles. Sew the H/I units to the sides of the block, referring to **Diagram 6** for placement. Add a J triangle to the bottom corner to complete the block.

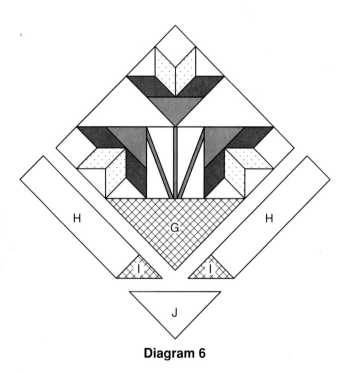

Diagram 6

7. To add sashing around the block, sew 14½-inch burgundy sashing strips to two opposite sides of a block. Press seam allowances toward the sashing strips.

8. Sew 18½-inch burgundy sashing strips to the remaining two sides of a block. Press seam allowances toward the sashing strips.

9. Repeat to make a total of four Lily Basket blocks with sashing.

Making the Garden Maze

1. Referring to **Diagram 7A,** pin a 2½-inch burgundy paisley sashing square to each end of a muslin sashing strip with right sides facing and raw edges aligned.

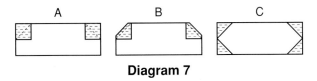

Diagram 7

2. Sew diagonally across each square as indicated by dashed lines on the diagram. Trim away the corners, leaving a ¼-inch seam allowance, as shown in **Diagram 7B.** Open out burgundy triangles and press seam allowances toward them. In a similar manner, sew squares to the bottom two corners of the muslin sashing strip. The finished sashing strip should look like **Diagram 7C.**

3. Repeat to make a total of four garden maze sashing strips.

4. As shown in the **Quilt Diagram,** lay out the blocks in two rows with garden maze sashing strips between the blocks and the 4½-inch burgundy paisley square in the quilt center.

5. Sew the pieces together in rows. Press seam allowances in alternate directions from row to row. Join the rows.

Adding the Borders

1. Center and sew a green stripe border to each muslin border. Press seam allowances toward the green borders.

2. Sew the borders to the quilt top. Your border strips will be longer than your quilt length. *Do not cut off excess fabric.* The extra length will be needed to miter the corners of the borders. Press the seam allowances toward the borders. Miter the border corner seams, referring to page 160 for more detailed directions.

Quilt Diagram

3. Referring to the **Quilt Diagram** and the photo on page 35, position and baste the bias border vine to the quilt borders, forming gentle curves. Appliqué the vine in place.

4. Appliqué a prepared lily unit at the center of each border.

5. Baste under the seam allowance on all X and Y diamonds to prepare them for appliqué.

6. Appliqué an X diamond and two Y diamonds at each corner of the border, as shown in the **Quilt Diagram.**

7. Appliqué four Y diamonds along each border, placing them along the inner curves of the vine.

Quilting and Finishing

1. Mark quilting designs onto the quilt top. The quilt shown was outline quilted ¼ inch from the edges of all pieces and has echo quilting in the muslin borders. A cable pattern from a com-

mercially produced quilt stencil was used for the burgundy sashing.

2. To piece the quilt back, divide the backing fabric into two 1¾-yard pieces. Cut one piece in half lengthwise. Sew a half panel to each long side of the full panel. Press the seam allowances toward the narrow panels.

3. Layer the quilt back, batting, and quilt top; baste. Trim the quilt back and batting so they are approximately 3 inches larger than the quilt top on all sides.

4. Quilt all marked designs, and add additional quilting if desired.

5. Make approximately 230 inches of French-fold binding from the burgundy solid fabric. See page 164 for instructions on making and attaching binding.

6. Sew the binding to the quilt top. Trim the excess batting and backing, and hand finish the binding to the wrong side of the quilt. If you wish to hang this quilt rather than use it as a tablecloth, refer to page 167 for instructions on attaching a hanging sleeve.

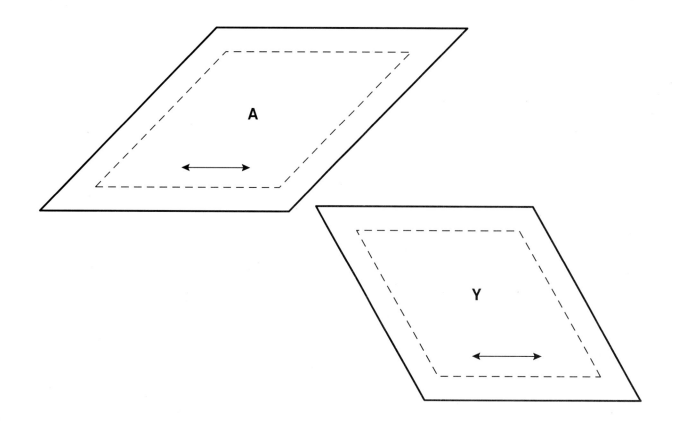

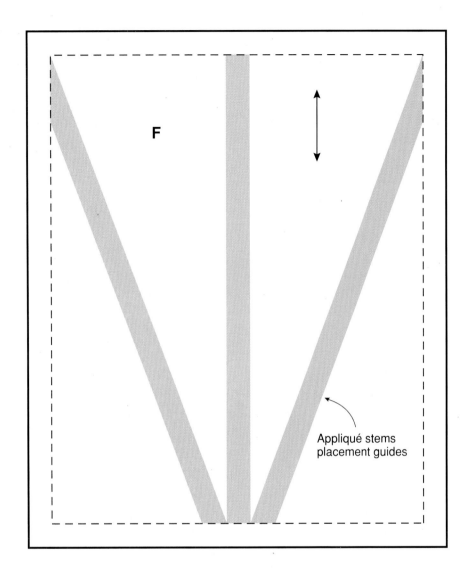

F

Appliqué stems
placement guides

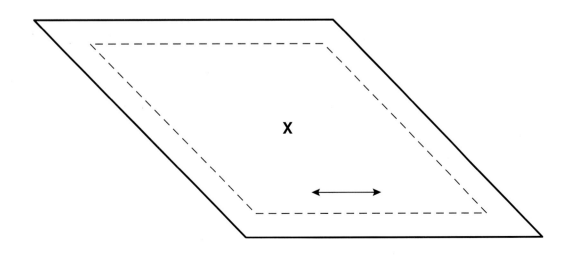

X

Duck Quilt

Quiltmaker: Teresa S. Hannaway

This handsome duck wallhanging is the perfect accessory to hang in an office or den. Teresa's interesting treatment of the borders and corners contrasts well with the appliqué detail. The project uses quick and easy techniques including fusible appliqué and machine satin stitch, so if you need a last-minute gift that doesn't look like one, here's one you can whip up in a weekend!

Skill Level: Easy

Size: Finished quilt is 34 × 23½ inches

Fabrics and Supplies

- ✓ ½ yard of dark green print fabric for narrow borders and duck head
- ✓ ½ yard of dark brown print fabric for middle border, duck's breast, tail, and eye, and cattails
- ✓ ¼ yard of medium green print fabric for border appliqués and cattail leaves
- ✓ ¼ yard of tan print fabric for lower background and duck bill
- ✓ ⅛ yard, or scraps, of gray-and-navy print fabric for border appliqués and duck back
- ✓ ⅛ yard, or scraps, of navy-and-cream print fabric for duck wing and neck band
- ✓ ⅓ yard of beige print fabric for upper background
- ✓ ¾ yard of fabric for quilt back
- ✓ ¾ yard of polyester fleece
- ✓ 1 yard of 22-inch-wide paper-backed fusible webbing
- ✓ 1 yard of tear-away stabilizer for machine appliqué
- ✓ Rotary cutter, ruler, and mat
- ✓ Thread to match the appliqué fabrics

Cutting

All measurements include ¼-inch seam allowances. Measurements for the outer borders are longer than the quilt dimensions. Do not trim off the extra fabric; it will be used to miter the border corners.

The instructions are written for quick-cutting the background and border pieces using a rotary cutter and a ruler. Cut all strips across the fabric width. Note that for some of the pieces, the quick-cutting method will result in leftover fabric.

The appliqué patterns are reversed from the finished quilt so you can trace them onto fusible webbing which will be fused to the wrong side of the fabric. Your finished project will end up looking like the one in the photograph. Following manufacturer's instructions, trace the appliqué shapes onto the paper side of the fusible webbing. Note: For the duck pieces, you will have to match the large dots on the two halves of the pattern to make a whole pattern. Fuse the webbing to the appropriate fabric, and cut out the pieces.

From the dark green print fabric, cut:
- Eight 1½-inch strips for the inner and outer borders; trim 4 strips to 36 inches and 4 strips to 25 inches
- 1 duck head

From the dark brown print fabric, cut:
- Four 3½-inch strips for the middle border; trim 2 strips to 36 inches and 2 strips to 25 inches
- 1 duck breast
- 1 duck tail
- 1 duck eye
- 4 cattails

From the medium green print fabric, cut:
- Four 5-inch squares for border appliqués
  Cut one 5 × 22-inch strip. Cut the strip into four 5-inch squares.
- 1 *each* of 6 different cattail leaves

From the tan print fabric, cut:
- One 5 × 24½-inch piece for lower background
- 1 duck bill

From the gray-and-navy print fabric, cut:
- Four 3-inch squares for border appliqués
- 1 duck back

From the navy-and-cream print fabric, cut:
- 1 duck wing
- 1 neck band

From the beige print fabric, cut:
- One 9½ × 24½-inch piece for upper background

Making the Inner Quilt

1. Sew the tan lower background piece to the beige upper background piece. Press the seam allowance toward the tan piece.

2. Referring to the **Quilt Diagram,** position the appliqué pieces on the background and fuse in place, overlapping adjoining pieces as necessary. Using a pencil or tailor's chalk and a ruler, draw the cattail stems.

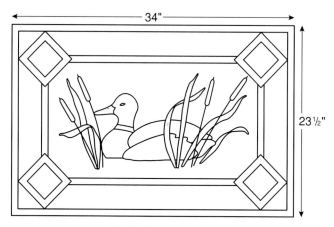

Quilt Diagram

3. Cut a piece of fabric stabilizer the size of the background and pin it to the wrong side of the background fabric. Machine satin stitch around all appliqué pieces using matching thread. Satin stitch the cattail stems as marked, using dark green thread. When stitching is complete, tear away the stabilizer. Instructions for machine appliqué are on page 158.

Adding the Borders

1. To make the top and bottom borders, sew 36-inch dark green strips to both long sides of each of the 36-inch dark brown strips. Press the seam allowances toward the brown strips.

2. In the same manner, make borders for the quilt sides using the 25-inch strips.

3. Sew the borders to the quilt center, treating each triple border as one border. Your border strips will be longer than your quilt length. *Do not cut off excess fabric.* The extra length will be needed to miter the corners of the borders. Press the seam allowances toward the borders. Miter the border corner seams, referring to page 160 for more detailed directions.

4. Referring to the **Quilt Diagram** for placement, fuse a medium green square to each corner of the quilt. Center and fuse a gray-and-navy print square on top of each green square.

5. Cut pieces of stabilizer to pin under the areas to be stitched. Machine satin stitch around the squares.

Finishing

1. Cut a 36 × 25-inch piece from the backing fabric and from the fleece.

2. Layer the quilt top, backing, and fleece. The first layer is the fleece, followed by the backing fabric with the right side facing up. The top layer is the quilt top with the right side facing down. Pin the layers together.

3. Sew the layers together, stitching ¼ inch from the quilt top edges and leaving an opening for turning. Trim the excess quilt back and fleece, leaving ¼-inch seam allowance. Trim the corners diagonally.

4. Turn the quilt right side out; stitch the opening closed.

5. Machine quilt in the ditch around the three borders. Add any additional quilting as desired. Refer to page 167 for instructions on making and adding a hanging sleeve.

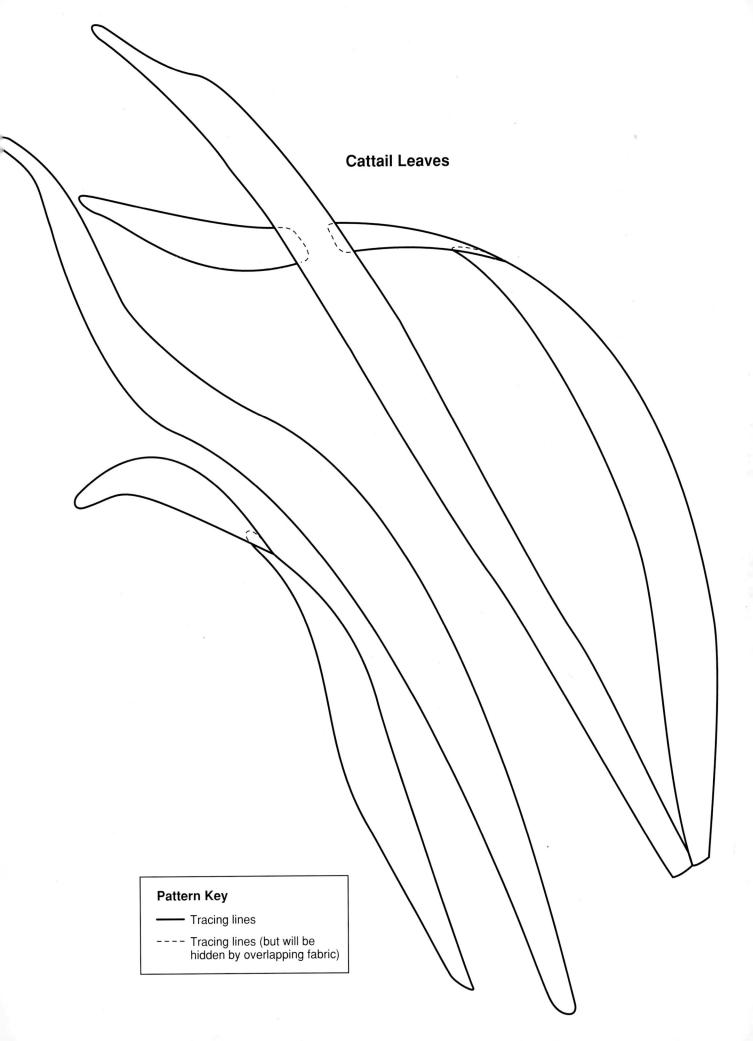

Cattail Leaves

Pattern Key

———— Tracing lines

- - - - Tracing lines (but will be
hidden by overlapping fabric)

Duck A Appliqué Pattern

Match dots with those on other half of pattern

Pattern Key

——— Tracing lines

- - - - Tracing lines (but will be hidden by overlapping fabric)

Duck B Appliqué Pattern

Match dots with those on other half of pattern

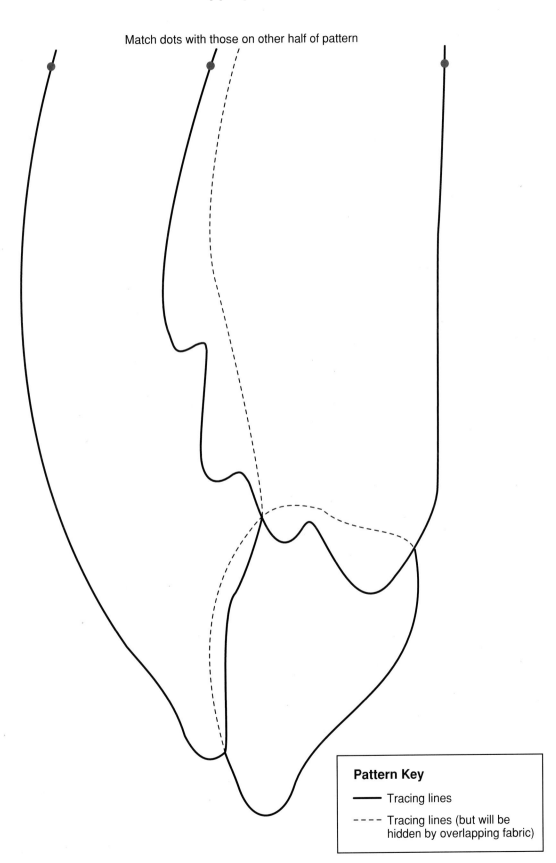

Pattern Key

——— Tracing lines

- - - - Tracing lines (but will be hidden by overlapping fabric)

Cattail and
Cattail Leaves

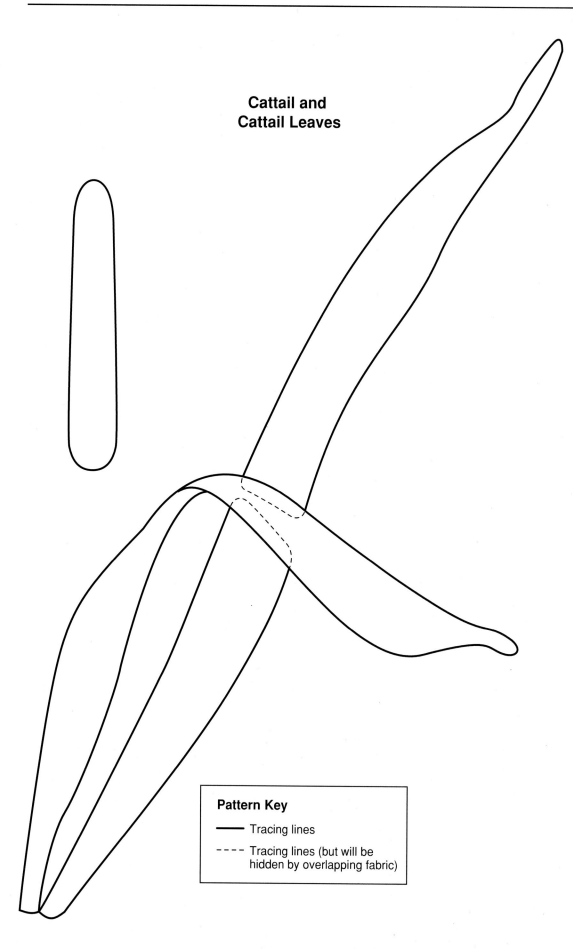

Pattern Key

——— Tracing lines

- - - - Tracing lines (but will be
hidden by overlapping fabric)

Tulips 'Round the Garden Path

Quiltmaker: Barbara Hammett

Pastel pink pathways weave their way through a delightful garden of floral print fabrics. While nearly a dozen fabrics are used to create the springtime garden, the colors come together nicely on the dark print garden background. And what could be prettier for a garden border than an abundance of appliqué tulips in full bloom?

Skill Level: Easy

Size: Finished quilt is 76 × 91 inches
Finished block is 15 inches square

Fabrics and Supplies

- ✓ 3½ yards of dark floral print fabric for the patchwork "garden" and binding
- ✓ 4 yards of pastel pink solid fabric for the border and "paths"
- ✓ ½ yard *each* of ten different medium floral print fabrics for the patchwork "flowers" and appliqué tulips
- ✓ ¼ yard *each* of two different green print fabrics for the appliqué leaves
- ✓ 6 yards of fabric for quilt back
- ✓ Queen-size quilt batting (90 × 108 inches)
- ✓ Rotary cutter, ruler, and mat
- ✓ Template plastic or plastic-coated freezer paper

Cutting

All measurements include ¼-inch seam allowances. Cut all strips across the fabric width unless directed otherwise. The measurements for the borders include several extra inches in length; trim them to the exact length before sewing them to the quilt top. Instructions are given for quick-cutting all of the pieces using a rotary cutter and a ruler except for the Tulip, Tulip Tip, and Leaf pattern pieces. Make templates for these appliqué pieces using the patterns on page 53. Note that for some of the pieces, the quick-cutting method will result in leftover fabric.

You may want to cut just enough pieces to make one block to test your templates, cutting, and seam allowances for accuracy. If your finished block does not measure the size stated above, you can make adjustments before cutting all your fabric.

From the dark floral print fabric, cut:
- 640 A triangles
  Cut twenty-seven 3⅜-inch strips. Cut these strips into 320 squares, each 3⅜ inches square. Cut each square in half diagonally to make two triangles.
- Nine 2-inch binding strips

From the pastel pink solid fabric, cut:
- Four 8½ × 80-inch borders *lengthwise*
- 400 A triangles
  Cut two 3⅜ × 80-inch strips *lengthwise*. From the strips cut 44 squares, each 3⅜ inches square. Cut thirteen 3⅜-inch strips *crosswise*. Cut these strips into 156 squares, each 3⅜ inches square. Cut each square in half diagonally to make two triangles.

From each of ten different medium floral print fabrics, cut:
- 24 A triangles
  Cut one 3⅜-inch strip. From the strip cut 12 squares, each 3⅜ inches square. Cut each square in half diagonally to make two triangles.
- 2 B squares
  Cut two 5½-inch squares.
- 3 Tulips
- 3 Tulip Tips

From each of two different green print fabrics, cut:
- 18 leaves and 18 reverse leaves

```
Fabric Key

[dark] Dark floral print

[white] Pastel pink solid

[gray] Medium floral prints
```

Piecing the Blocks

1. Sew a dark floral A triangle to a pastel pink A triangle along the long edges to form a triangle-square as shown at the left in **Diagram 1.** Press the seam allowance toward the dark fabric. Make 400 triangle-squares.

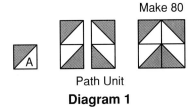

Make 80

Path Unit
Diagram 1

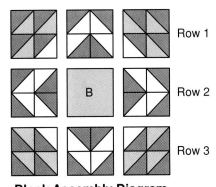

Row 1

Row 2

Row 3

Block Assembly Diagram

2. Referring to the **Fabric Key** and **Diagram 1,** lay out four triangle-squares. Pay careful attention to the angle of the diagonal seams and the placement of the light and dark triangles. Sew the units in two vertical rows with two units in each row. Press the seam allowances in opposite directions in the two rows. Join the rows; press the seam allowance to one side. Make a total of 80 Path Units. Reserve the remaining triangle-square units for the Flower Units.

3. Sew a medium floral A triangle to a dark floral A triangle along the long edges to form a triangle-square as shown at the left in **Diagram 2.** Press the seam allowance toward the dark fabric. Make 240 triangle-squares, 24 from each floral fabric.

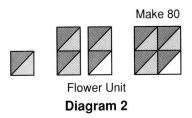

Make 80

Flower Unit
Diagram 2

4. Referring to **Diagram 2,** lay out three triangle-squares with matching floral fabric and one triangle-square unit with pastel pink fabric. Pay careful attention to the angle of the diagonal seams and the placement of the light and dark triangles. Sew the units in two vertical rows of two units. Press the seam allowances in opposite directions in the two rows. Join the rows; press the seam allowance to one side. Make a total of 80 Flower Units, 8 units from each floral fabric.

5. To make one block, lay out four matching Flower Units, one B square from the matching floral fabric, and four Path Units as shown in the **Block Assembly Diagram.**

6. Join the pieces to create three horizontal rows as shown in the **Block Assembly Diagram.** Press the seam allowances in alternate directions from row to row. Join the rows. Press the seams to one side. The completed block should measure 15½ inches square, including seam allowances. Make a total of 20 Garden Path blocks, two from each of the floral fabrics.

Assembling the Quilt Top

1. Referring to the **Quilt Diagram,** lay out the blocks in five horizontal rows with four blocks in each row. Arrange the blocks to achieve a pleasing color balance.

2. Join blocks in rows. Press the seam allowances in alternate directions from row to row. Join the rows. Press the seam allowances to one side.

3. Measure the quilt from top to bottom through the center. Trim two borders to this length (approximately 75½ inches). Sew the borders to the sides of the quilt top.

4. Measure the width of the quilt, including the side borders, through the center of the quilt. Trim the remaining two borders to this length (approximately 76½ inches). Sew the borders to the top and bottom edges of the quilt top.

Appliquéing the Border Tulips

1. Refer to page 156 for instructions on how to prepare appliqué pieces. The freezer paper appliqué method explained on page 157 is well suited for this project. You may also want to

Quilt Diagram

refer to "Five-Step Machine Appliqué" on page 11 for tips on invisible machine appliqué.

2. Referring to the photo on page 49 for placement, pin or baste tulips, tips, and leaves to borders. Hand or machine appliqué the pieces to the borders.

Quilting and Finishing

1. Mark quilting designs onto the quilt top with a pencil or other removable marking tool. The quilting designs used in the Path Units and block center squares on the quilt shown are on the opposite page. The quilt shown also has a diagonal grid of 1-inch squares quilted in the background of the borders.

2. To piece the quilt back, divide the backing fabric into two 3-yard pieces and trim the selvages. Divide one of the 3-yard pieces in half

lengthwise. Sew a half panel to each long side of the full-width panel. Press the seam allowances toward the outer panels.

3. Layer the quilt back, batting, and quilt top; baste. Trim the quilt back and batting so they are approximately 3 inches larger than the quilt top on all sides.

4. Quilt all marked designs by hand or machine, and add additional quilting as desired. The quilt shown was outline quilted around the appliqué pieces and quilted in the ditch around the patchwork shapes.

5. Make approximately 360 inches of French-fold binding by joining the dark floral binding strips with diagonal seams. See page 164 for instructions on making and attaching binding.

6. Sew the binding to the quilt top. Trim the excess batting and backing, and hand finish the binding on the wrong side of the quilt.

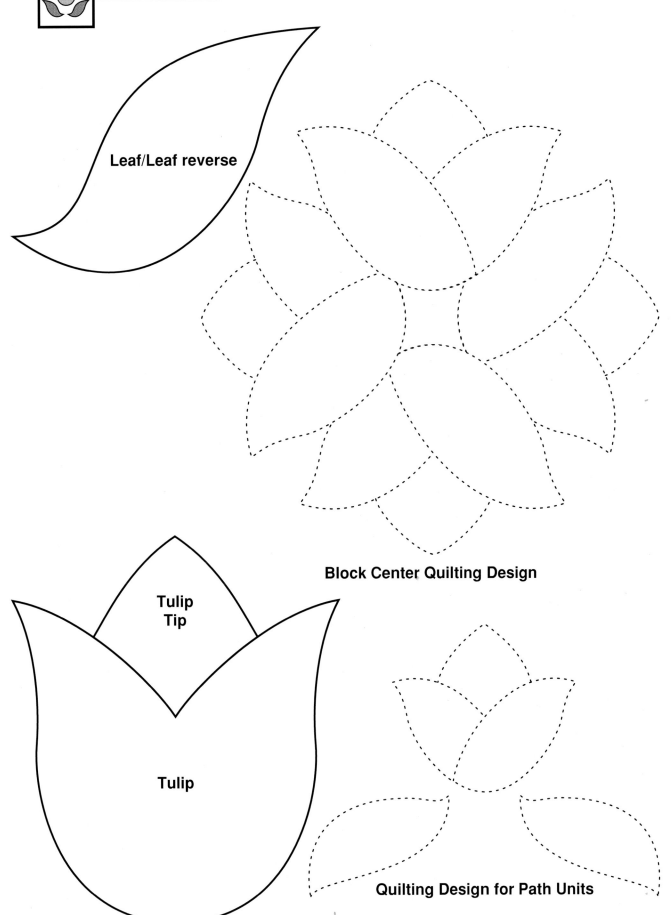

Leaf/Leaf reverse

Block Center Quilting Design

Tulip Tip

Tulip

Quilting Design for Path Units

Patchwork Needle Case

Quiltmaker: Kathy Berschneider

Three patchwork spool blocks neatly wrap up your quilting necessities in this handy traveling case. Once your quilting companions see how cute and convenient this little sewing pocket is, they'll surely all want one. So plan ahead and make several in a variety of color combinations—for yourself and as gifts for your friends.

Skill Level: Easy

Size: Finished case is 15 × 6 inches opened; 4¾ × 6 inches closed

Fabrics and Supplies

- ✓ ¼ yard of muslin for foundations
- ✓ ¼ yard of navy blue floral print fabric for interior and front of case and patchwork blocks
- ✓ ⅛ yard, or scraps, of pink print fabric for patchwork
- ✓ ⅛ yard, or scraps, of cream print fabric for patchwork, needle keeper, and scissors pocket
- ✓ One 5½-inch piece of ½-inch-wide black Velcro hook-and-loop fastener
- ✓ One 6-inch piece of ¼-inch-wide elastic
- ✓ ½ yard of ¼-inch-wide sateen ribbon
- ✓ One 3 × 2½-inch scrap of low-loft quilt batting to line needle keeper
- ✓ Rotary cutter, ruler, and mat
- ✓ Template plastic

Cutting

All measurements include a ¼-inch seam allowance. Instructions given are for rotary cutting pieces for the needle case and many of the patchwork pieces. Cut all strips across the fabric width. Make templates for pieces D, F, G, and K from the patterns on pages 57–58. Also make a paper pattern for the scissors pocket.

From the muslin, cut:
- Two 6½ × 15½-inch foundation pieces

From the navy blue floral print fabric, cut:
- One 6½ × 15½-inch piece for interior of case
- Two 1½ × 15½-inch strips for front of case
- Four 1¼ × 4½-inch strips for front of case
- 2 B rectangles for Spool Patch block
  Cut one 1½ × 5-inch strip. Cut the strip into two 1½ × 2½-inch rectangles.

- 4 C triangles for Spool Patch block
  Cut two 1⅞-inch squares. Cut each square in half diagonally into two triangles.
- 2 E triangles for Twisted-Thread Spool block
  Cut one 4¼-inch square. Cut the square in half diagonally both ways into four triangles. You will have two extra triangles.
- 2 G pieces for Twisted-Thread Spool block
- 2 I rectangles for Wooden Spool block
  Cut one 1½ × 4-inch strip. Cut the strip into 1½ × 2-inch rectangles.
- 4 J triangles for Wooden Spool block
  Cut two 2⅜-inch squares. Cut each square in half diagonally into two triangles.

From the pink print fabric, cut:
- 1 A square for Spool Patch block
  Cut one 2½-inch square.
- 1 E triangle for Twisted-Thread Spool block
  Cut one 4¼-inch square. Cut the square in half diagonally both ways into four triangles. You will have three extra triangles.
- 1 F piece for Twisted-Thread Spool block

From the cream print fabric, cut:
- 2 D pieces for Spool Patch block
- 1 E triangle for Twisted-Thread Spool block
  Cut one 4¼-inch square. Cut the square in half diagonally both ways into four triangles. You will have three extra triangles.
- 1 F piece for Twisted-Thread Spool block
- 1 H square for Wooden Spool block
  Cut one 1½-inch square.
- 2 K pieces for Wooden Spool block
- One 3½ × 3-inch rectangle for needle keeper
- 2 scissors pocket pieces

Making the Spool Blocks

Referring to the **Fabric Key** and **Block Piecing Diagram** on page 56, lay out the pieces for each of the blocks. Join the pieces into rows, pressing seam allowances toward darker fabrics whenever possible.

1. For the Spool Patch, sew the C triangles to the short ends of each D piece for the top and bottom rows. Sew the B rectangles to opposite sides of the A square for the middle row. Join the three rows together to complete the block.

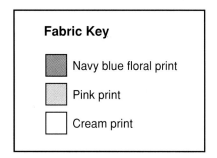

Fabric Key

Navy blue floral print

Pink print

Cream print

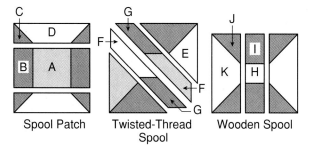

Spool Patch   Twisted-Thread Spool   Wooden Spool

Block Piecing Diagram

2. For the Twisted-Thread Spool, sew a navy floral print and a pink print E triangle together to form a large right triangle. In the same manner, join a floral print and a cream print E triangle. To make the thread sections, sew a cream F piece to a floral print G piece. Sew a pink print F piece to a floral print G piece. Sew the two F/G sections together, referring to the **Block Piecing Diagram** for color placement. Sew the E triangle units to either side of the thread units, again referring to the diagram for placement.

3. For the Wooden Spool, sew a J triangle to the diagonal edges of the two K pieces. These will form the left and right sides of the block. To make the center row, sew an I rectangle to the top and bottom of the H square, as shown in the diagram. Sew the three rows together to complete the block.

Assembling the Front of the Needle Case

1. Referring to the **Front Needle Case Diagram,** join the three blocks and the four 1¼-

inch navy floral print strips to form a horizontal row. Press the seams toward the strips.

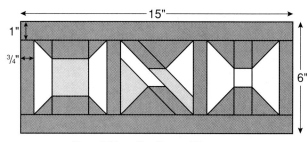

Front Needle Case Diagram

2. Sew the two 15½-inch navy floral strips to the top and bottom of the row to complete the front of the needle case. Press the seams toward the strips.

3. Place the front of the needle case atop one of the muslin foundation pieces. Machine quilt as desired, stitching the front of the needle case and the muslin together. The needle case pictured was machine quilted in the ditch around each spool.

Assembling the Interior of the Needle Case

1. Lay the navy blue floral rectangle atop the remaining muslin foundation piece with the right side of the fabric facing you. Machine quilt approximately five horizontal lines of stitching about 1 inch apart across the rectangle.

2. Cut both the hook and the loop sections of your Velcro strip in half. Referring to the **Interior Needle Case Diagram,** topstitch the four hook and loop Velcro pieces in place.

3. Pin the piece of elastic to the left section of the needle case, centering the elastic between the two Velcro strips as shown in the **Interior Needle Case Diagram.** Turn under the ends and stitch through all layers at each end to tack the elastic in place. To make the thread spool loops, stitch the elastic to the needle case at two other points, approximately 1⅛ inches from each end of the elastic. While your stitching will be about 1⅛ inches apart, you should have approximately 1½ inches of elastic in each loop so you have room to slip in your spools.

Dotted lines indicate stitching lines.

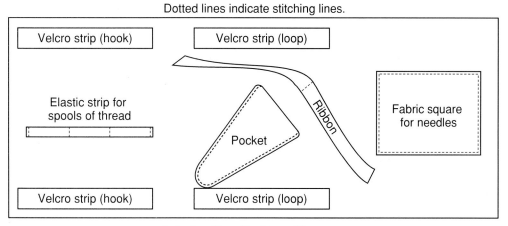

Interior Needle Case Diagram

4. Place the two scissors pocket pieces right sides together. Stitch around the outside edges, leaving an opening along one of the long edges for turning. Clip, turn right side out, and press flat (tucking in the unstitched edges along the seam line). Position the pocket in the center section of the needle case as shown in the diagram and top stitch along the edge. Leave the top of the pocket open for the scissors.

5. Trim the ribbon to 16 inches. Position the ribbon above the pocket and machine stitch through the middle point of the ribbon to hold the scissors tie in place.

6. Fold and press under a scant ¼-inch seam allowance on the rectangle of fabric for the needle keeper. Place the batting scrap against the wrong side of the rectangle, tucking it inside the folded seam allowances. Position and stitch the rectangle to the right-hand section of the needle case as shown in the diagram, topstitching close to the folded edge.

Finishing

1. Place the front and interior sections of the needle case right sides together. Stitch around the outside edges, leaving a 3-inch section open for turning.

2. Turn to right side and press, avoiding Velcro strips. Hand stitch opening closed.

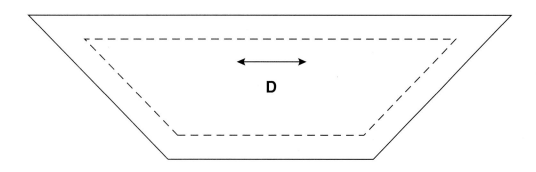

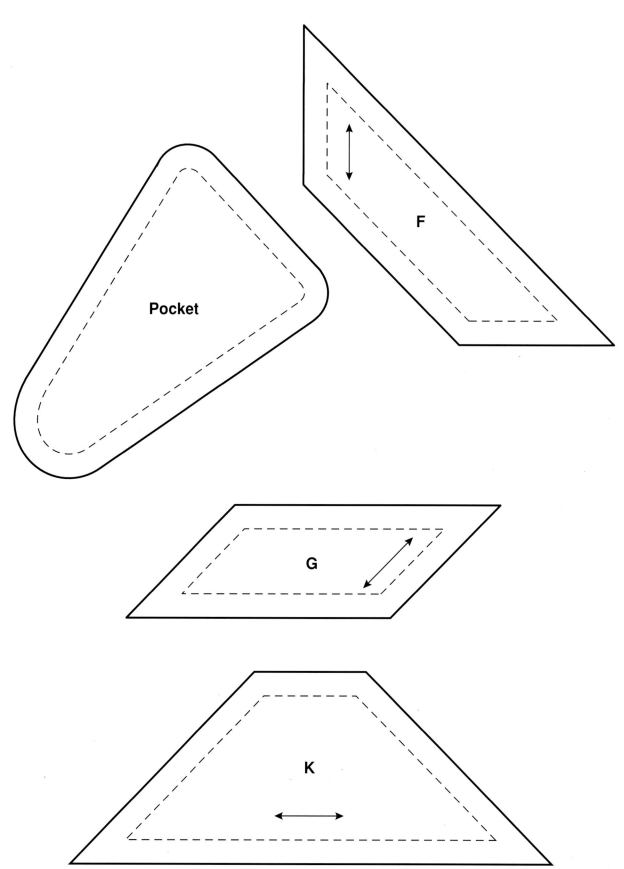

Oak Leaf and Reel

Quiltmaker: Melva Betka

This classic red and green appliqué pattern works well in today's sophisticated prints and updated tones of teal and cranberry. Melva framed the 13 large appliqué blocks in a traditional Garden Maze setting for extra interest. And her distinctive oak leaf and acorn quilting designs add the final graceful touch to a simply beautiful quilt.

Skill Level: Intermediate

Size: Finished quilt is approximately 86½ inches square
Finished block is 15 inches square (approximately 21¼ inches on the diagonal)
Finished setting square is 3½ inches square (approximately 5 inches on the diagonal)

Fabrics and Supplies

✓ 5 yards of beige print fabric for background squares and setting triangles

✓ 4¾ yards of dark teal paisley fabric for sashing, border, appliqués, and binding

✓ 2 yards of cranberry solid fabric for sashing and border

✓ 1 yard of cranberry-and-black print fabric for appliqués

✓ 2¾ yards of 90-inch-wide fabric for quilt back

✓ Queen-size quilt batting (90 × 108 inches)

✓ Rotary cutter, ruler, and mat

✓ Plastic-coated freezer paper or template plastic

✓ Tracing paper

✓ Black permanent marker

Cutting

All measurements include a ¼-inch seam allowance. The instructions are written for quick-cutting the background squares, sashing strips, border strips, and some of the setting square pieces with a rotary cutter and ruler. Cut all strips across the fabric width unless instructed otherwise. For the Garden Maze sashing, you will cut lengthwise strips to make strip sets for quicker piecing.

Patterns for A, B, and C appliqué pieces and the D, E, and F patchwork pieces begin on page 64. The appliqué patterns are finished size; add seam allowances when you cut the pieces from fabric. Read through the tips in "Hand Appliqué" beginning on page 156 and choose the appliqué method you wish to use for the blocks. Either make plastic templates to mark and cut the appliqué pieces or make freezer paper templates. Patchwork patterns indicate cut size as well as finished size.

You may want to cut just enough pieces to make one block to test your templates, cutting, and seam allowances for accuracy.

From the beige print fabric, cut:
• Thirteen 15½-inch background squares
Cut seven 15½-inch strips. Cut the strips into 15½-inch squares.

• 8 side setting triangles
Cut two 24-inch squares. Cut each square in half diagonally in both directions to make four triangles. Note: These triangles and the corner setting triangles are cut larger than needed. They will be trimmed to size after the quilt is assembled.

• 4 corner setting triangles
Cut two 12½-inch squares. Cut each square in half diagonally to make two triangles.

From the dark teal paisley fabric, cut one 48-inch length. From this piece, cut:
• 12 *lengthwise* strips for strip sets, each 3 × 48 inches

From the remaining paisley fabric, cut two 22-inch lengths. From these two pieces, cut:
• 16 *lengthwise* border strips, each 4¼ × 22 inches

From the remaining paisley fabric, cut:
• 72 F triangles for pieced setting squares
Use Template F
OR
Cut two 3¾-inch strips. From these strips, cut 18 squares, each 3¾ inches square. Cut each square in half diagonally in both directions to make four triangles.

• 52 B appliqué leaves

• Reserve the remaining fabric for binding

From the cranberry solid fabric, cut one 48-inch length. From this piece, cut:
• 24 *lengthwise* strips for strip sets, each 1 × 48 inches

From the remaining cranberry solid fabric, cut:
• 24 D pieces for pieced setting squares

• 36 E pieces for pieced setting squares

- 12 border squares
  Cut two 4¼-inch strips. Cut the strips into twelve 4¼-inch squares.

From the cranberry-and-black print fabric, cut:
- 13 A appliqué pieces
- 52 C appliqué pieces

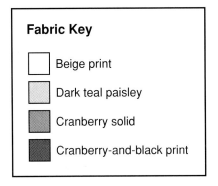

Fabric Key

☐ Beige print

☐ Dark teal paisley

☐ Cranberry solid

☐ Cranberry-and-black print

Making the Blocks

1. Make a master pattern for the appliqué design to use as a guide for positioning the appliqué pieces on the background squares. Fold a large sheet of tracing paper in half both ways. Refer to the **Block Diagram** and trace around templates or patterns to make a full-size drawing of the block. Darken the pattern outlines with a permanent marker.

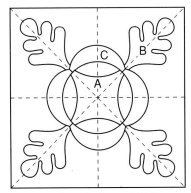

Dotted lines indicate fold lines
Block Diagram

2. To make one block, fold a beige fabric square in half vertically, horizontally, and diagonally in both directions. Crease lightly. Center

the master appliqué pattern under the fabric square; pin the fabric square to the paper one.

3. Use crease lines and the master pattern to help position an A appliqué piece at the center of the background square; pin the appliqué in place, pinning only through the two fabrics. Unpin the background square from the paper master pattern. Appliqué the A piece in place.

4. In the same manner, position, pin, and appliqué the four B oak leaves in place. Make sure, as you position the appliqués, that the C pieces will overlap and cover the section where A and B pieces meet. Position and appliqué the C pieces last.

5. Repeat to make a total of 13 blocks.

Making the Garden Maze Sashing and Setting Squares

1. Referring to **Diagram 1** and the **Fabric Key,** stitch a 1-inch cranberry solid strip to each long side of the twelve 3-inch teal paisley strips. Press the seams toward the cranberry strips. Cut each of the 12 strip sets into three 15½-inch sections.

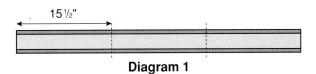

15½"

Diagram 1

2. Sew a teal paisley F triangle to each long side of a cranberry solid E piece, as shown in **Diagram 2.** Repeat to make 36 units.

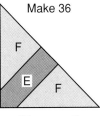

Make 36

Diagram 2

3. Referring to **Diagram 3,** sew the units made in Step 2 to opposite sides of 12 cranberry solid D pieces to make 12 sashing squares. Press seams toward the D pieces. You will have 12 **Diagram 2** units left over.

Make 12

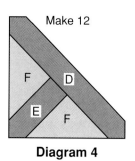

Diagram 3

4. To make the 12 sashing triangles for the outside edges, sew each of the 12 remaining triangle units to one side of the 12 remaining cranberry solid D pieces as shown in **Diagram 4.**

Make 12

Diagram 4

Assembling the Inner Quilt Top

1. Construct the vertical rows for the center section of the quilt by referring to **Diagram 5.** Three of the rows will have three blocks and four sashing sections per row. The other rows consist of three sashing sections and four pieced sashing squares or sashing triangles per row. Pay close attention to the diagram as you construct the rows. Press seams toward the sashing sections. Join the rows, matching sashing intersections.

Diagram 5

2. The corner units are constructed as shown in **Diagram 6.** Sew a sashing section to two opposite sides of an Oak Leaf block. Sew two sashing triangles to the ends of another sashing section, referring to the diagram for placement. Sew this sashing piece to the third side of the Oak Leaf block. Attach the side setting triangles to the Oak Leaf block. Press seams toward triangles. Sew a corner triangle to the block to complete a corner unit. The side setting triangles and corner triangles were cut larger than needed. As you construct the corner units, trim the outside edges of the setting pieces even with the raw edges of the sashing triangles as needed to square off the corner unit. Repeat to make four corner units.

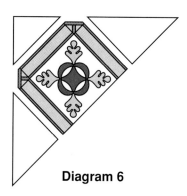

Diagram 6

3. Referring to the **Quilt Diagram,** sew corner units to two opposite sides of the quilt center section. The center section is shaded in the diagram. Sew the remaining corner units to the other sides of the quilt center. Press seams toward the center section.

Adding the Borders

1. Each border section contains four $4\frac{1}{4} \times$ 22-inch teal paisley strips separated by three cranberry solid border squares. Make four such border strips. Lay a border strip next to an edge of the inner quilt top. If necessary, adjust seams in the border strip so that the cranberry squares line up with the sashing triangles. Repeat for the remaining three borders.

2. Sew the borders to the quilt top. Your border strips will be longer than your quilt length. *Do not cut off excess fabric.* The extra length will be needed to miter the corners of the borders. Press the seam allowances toward the

borders. Miter the border corner seams, referring to page 160 for more detailed directions.

Quilting and Finishing

1. Mark desired quilting designs on the quilt top. The pattern for the leaf design is printed on the appliqué pattern on page 65. Oak leaves and acorns are quilted in the sashing, side setting triangles, and corner triangles. The quilt shown also has cross-hatching quilting in the background of the appliqué squares.

2. Cut the backing fabric into three equal lengths. Remove selvages and sew the three pieces together along the long edges. Press the seams away from the center panel.

3. Layer the quilt back, batting, and quilt top; baste. Trim the backing and batting so they are approximately 3 inches larger than the quilt top.

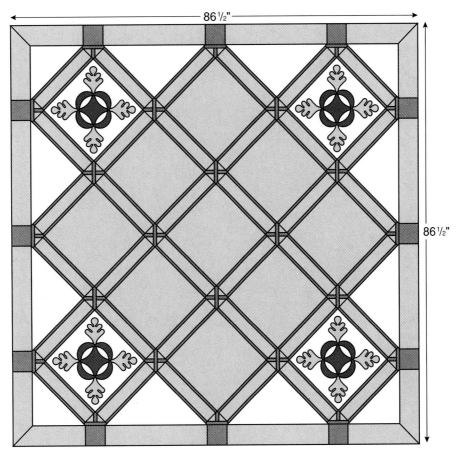

Quilt Diagram

4. Quilt all marked designs, and add additional quilting as desired, such as outline quilting for the appliqué pieces.

5. From the paisley fabric, make approximately 365 inches of binding. See page 164 for suggested binding widths and instructions on making and attaching binding. The quilt shown has a wider than normal binding, finishing approximately ¾ inch wide. For this type of binding, cut 2-inch-wide single-fold binding.

6. Sew the binding to the quilt top. Trim the excess batting and backing. If finishing with wide binding, trim batting and backing so raw edges extend ¾ inch from the machine stitching. Fold binding over extended batting and backing, and hand finish on the back of the quilt.

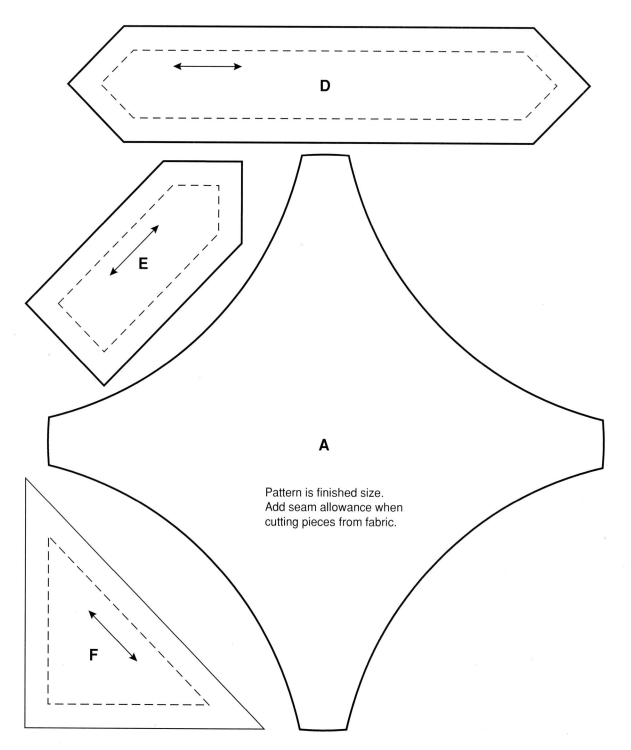

D

E

A

Pattern is finished size.
Add seam allowance when
cutting pieces from fabric.

F

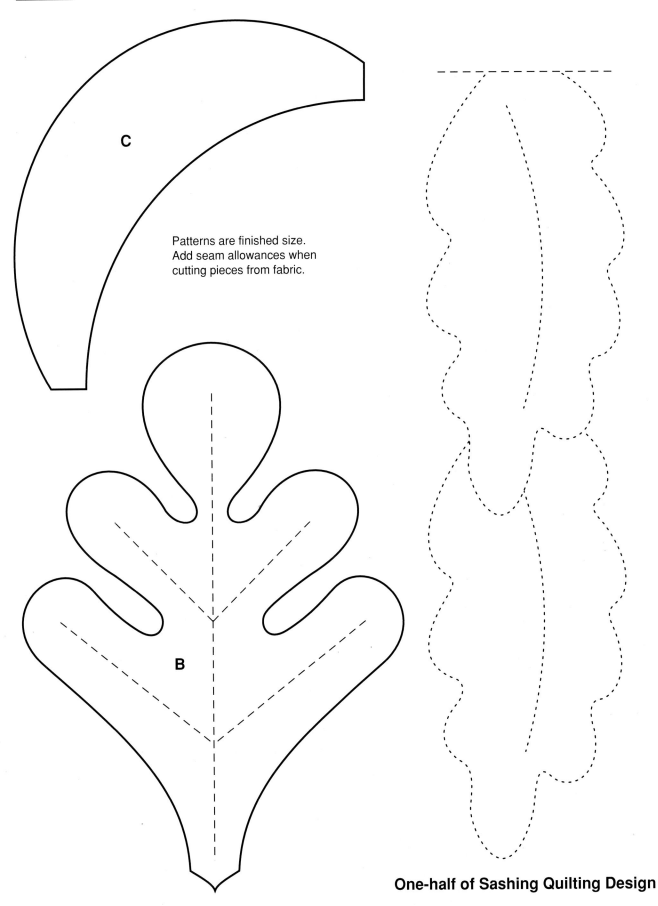

C

Patterns are finished size.
Add seam allowances when
cutting pieces from fabric.

B

One-half of Sashing Quilting Design

Pisces

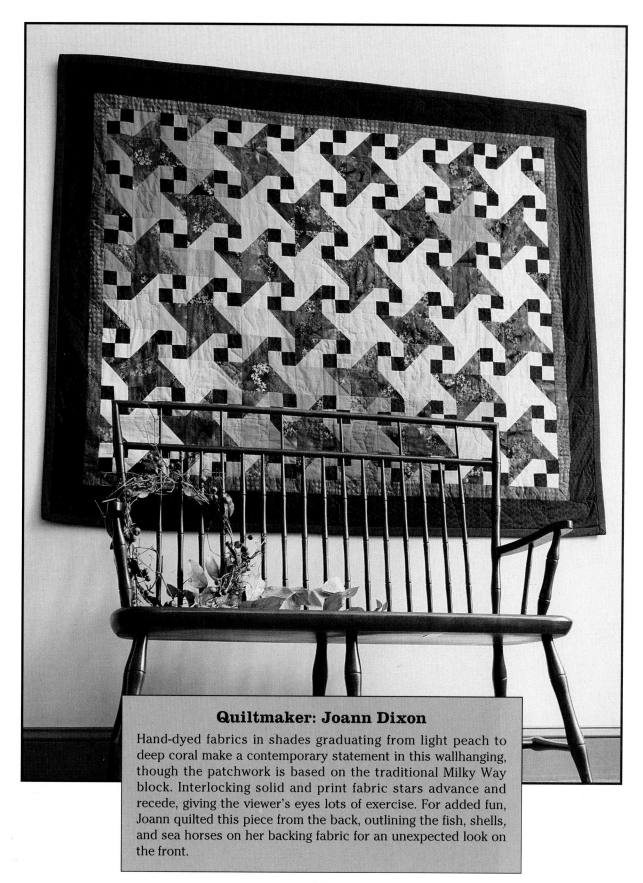

Quiltmaker: Joann Dixon

Hand-dyed fabrics in shades graduating from light peach to deep coral make a contemporary statement in this wallhanging, though the patchwork is based on the traditional Milky Way block. Interlocking solid and print fabric stars advance and recede, giving the viewer's eyes lots of exercise. For added fun, Joann quilted this piece from the back, outlining the fish, shells, and sea horses on her backing fabric for an unexpected look on the front.

66

Skill Level: Easy

Size: Finished quilt is 62 × 50 inches

Fabrics and Supplies

- ✓ 1½ yards of dark blue print fabric for outer border and patchwork
- ✓ 1⅛ yards of floral batik print fabric for patchwork
- ✓ ¼ yard *each* of five solid fabrics for patchwork, graduating in shade from pale peach to bright coral (Many quilt shops now carry commercially made hand-dyed fabrics. Or you can substitute traditional solid fabrics.)
- ✓ ⅜ yard of checked batik print fabric for inner border
- ✓ ½ yard of fabric for binding
- ✓ 3¼ yards of fabric for quilt back
- ✓ Twin-size quilt batting (72 × 90 inches)
- ✓ Rotary cutter, ruler, and mat

Cutting

All measurements include a ¼-inch seam allowance. The instructions are written for quick-cutting the pieces with a rotary cutter and ruler. Cut all strips across the fabric width. If you prefer to cut the pieces for the patchwork in a traditional manner, make templates for pieces A, B, and C. Patterns are on page 69.

From the dark blue print fabric, cut:
- Seven 4½-inch strips for outer border
- 126 A squares
  Use Template A
  OR
  Cut six 2-inch strips. Cut the strips into 2-inch squares.

From the floral batik fabric, cut:
- 110 B triangles
  Use Template B
  OR
  Cut six 3⅞-inch strips. Cut the strips into 55 squares, each 3⅞ inches square. Cut each

square in half diagonally to make two triangles.
- 24 C squares
  Use Template C
  OR
  Cut two 3½-inch strips. Cut the strips into 3½-inch squares.

From the five graduated coral fabrics, cut the following total numbers of pieces. Cut approximately the same number of pieces from each shade.
- 126 A squares
  Use Template A
  OR
  Cut six 2-inch strips. Cut the strips into 2-inch squares.
- 110 B triangles
  Use Template B
  OR
  Cut six 3⅞-inch strips. Cut the strips into 55 squares, each 3⅞ inches square. Cut each square in half diagonally to make two triangles.
- 24 C squares
  Use Template C
  OR
  Cut two 3½-inch strips. Cut the strips into 3½-inch squares.

From the checked batik fabric, cut:
- Five 2-inch strips for inner border

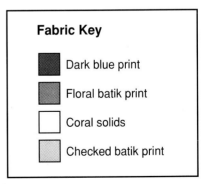

Laying Out and Piecing the Quilt

1. Referring to the **Fabric Key** and the **Quilt Diagram** on page 68, lay out all the pieces for the quilt. Position the various graduated coral squares and triangles as desired to form lighter and darker areas.

Tip: *For best results, pin or tape a piece of flannel or low-loft batting to the wall, and "stick" the quilt pieces to it. Stand back and view the quilt to make sure you like your arrangement of light and dark areas before you begin to sew.* ★

  2. Join the dark blue A squares and coral A squares as shown in **Diagram 1.** Press the seam allowances toward the blue fabric. Join two of these units to make a four-patch square. Repeat to make 63 four-patch squares, sewing one square at a time and replacing it in your layout as you work.

  3. Join the floral batik B triangles and coral B triangles to make 110 triangle-square units. See **Diagram 2.** Press seam allowances toward the darker fabric.

  4. Join the four-patch squares, the triangle-squares, and the C squares in 13 horizontal rows, referring to the **Quilt Diagram** for placement. Press seams in opposite directions from row to row. Join the rows.

Make 63

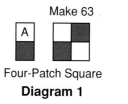

Four-Patch Square
Diagram 1

Make 110

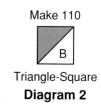

Triangle-Square
Diagram 2

Adding the Borders

  1. To make the inner border, cut one of the checked batik border strips in half. Sew each half strip to a full strip to make the top and bottom borders.

  2. To make the outer border, sew two dark blue strips together to make the top and bottom borders. To make the side borders, cut one border strip in half. Sew a half strip to each of the two remaining full strips.

  3. Press each of the borders in half to make a centering crease. Matching crease lines, join pairs of batik and dark blue borders to make four double borders.

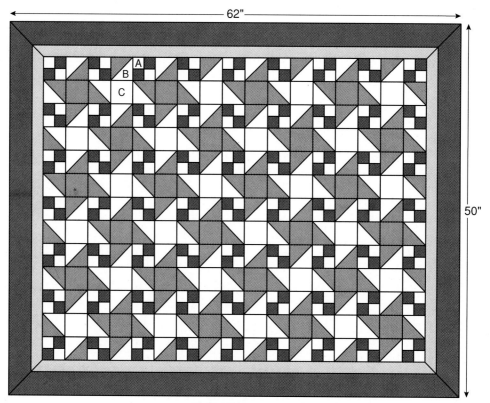

Quilt Diagram

4. Sew the borders to the quilt top. Your border strips will be longer than your quilt length. *Do not cut off excess fabric.* The extra length will be needed to miter the corners of the borders. Press the seam allowances toward the borders. Miter the border corner seams, referring to page 160 for more detailed directions.

Quilting and Finishing

1. Mark quilting designs as desired. For the quilt shown, an ocean print fabric was used for backing. Quilting was done from the wrong side, outlining the printed motifs in the fabric. Fish, sea horses, shells, and starfish appear at random on the quilt front.

2. Cut the backing fabric into two equal lengths. Trim off selvages. Sew the two pieces together. Press the seams in one direction.

3. Layer the quilt back, batting, and quilt top; baste. Trim the quilt back and batting so they are approximately 3 inches larger than the quilt top on all sides.

4. Quilt all marked designs.

5. From the binding fabric, make approximately 250 inches of binding. The quilt shown has a wider than normal binding, finishing approximately ¾ inch wide. For this type of binding, cut 2-inch, single-fold binding. For directions on making and attaching single-fold binding, see page 164.

6. Sew the binding to the quilt top. Trim the excess batting and backing. If finishing with wide binding, trim batting and backing so raw edges extend ¾ inch from machine stitching. Fold binding over extended batting and backing and hand finish on the wrong side of the quilt. See page 167 for instructions for making and attaching a hanging sleeve.

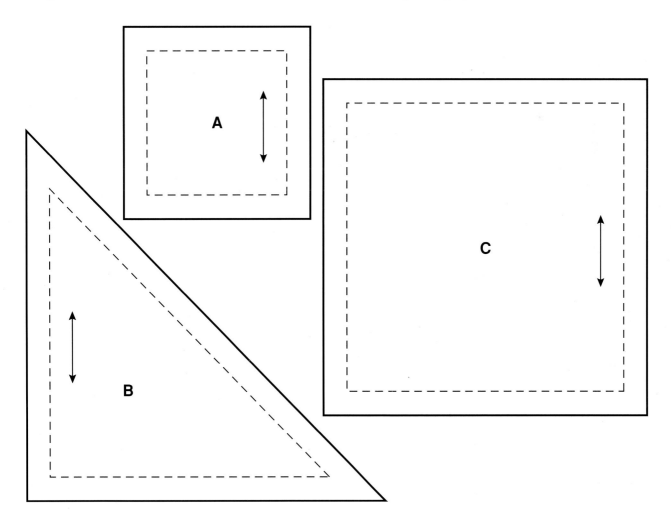

Special Feature

STAR QUILTS

California Star

Skill Level: Challenging

Size: Finished quilt is approximately 84 inches square

Fabrics and Supplies

✓ 3 yards of Fabric #1 (yellow solid) for patchwork

✓ ¾ yard of Fabric #2 (blue-and-yellow print) for patchwork

✓ 3 yards of Fabric #3 (brown paisley stripe) for middle border and patchwork. (Stripe for quilt border must repeat at least four times across the width of the fabric.)

✓ 1 yard of Fabric #4 (gold print) for patchwork

✓ 1¼ yards of Fabric #5 (dark blue and medium blue print) for patchwork

✓ 2½ yards of Fabric #6 (blue-and-black print) for patchwork, inner and outer borders, and binding

✓ 7½ yards of fabric for quilt back

✓ Queen-size quilt batting (90 × 108 inches)

✓ Rotary cutter, ruler, and mat

✓ Template plastic

Cutting

All measurements include ¼-inch seam allowances. Measurements for the outer borders are longer than the quilt dimensions. Do not trim off the extra fabric; it will be used to miter the border corners.

The instructions are written for quick-cutting the pieces for the large broken star using a rotary cutter and a ruler. Cut all strips across the fabric unless directed otherwise. For some pieces, the quick-cutting method will result in leftover fabric.

The diamonds for the small corner stars are cut and pieced traditionally using pattern piece B on page 77. When cutting the pieces from the border stripe (Fabric #3), position the template so all of the B diamonds are cut from the same part of the stripe. Instructions for making and

using templates are on page 153. You may want to cut just enough pieces to make one star point to test your template, cutting, and seam allowances for accuracy.

From Fabric #1 (yellow solid), cut:

- 64 A diamonds
  Cut four 1¾-inch strips for strip sets.

- 16 F squares
  Cut six 11-inch strips. Cut the strips into 16 squares, each 11 inches square.

- 8 E triangles
  Cut two 16-inch squares. Cut each square in half diagonally in both directions to make four triangles.

- 16 C triangles
  Cut four 5½-inch squares. Cut each square in half diagonally in both directions to make four triangles.

- 16 D squares
  Cut two 3½-inch strips. Cut the strips into 16 squares, each 3½ inches square.

From Fabric #2 (blue-and-yellow print), cut:

- 128 A diamonds
  Cut eight 1¾-inch strips for strip sets.

- 32 B diamonds

From Fabric #3 (brown paisley stripe), cut:

- Four 4¾ × 90-inch border strips cut *lengthwise* from matching fabric stripes

- 192 A diamonds
  Cut twelve 1¾-inch strips for strip sets.

- 64 B diamonds

From Fabric #4 (gold print), cut:

- 256 A diamonds
  Cut sixteen 1¾-inch strips for strip sets.

From Fabric #5 (dark blue and medium blue print), cut:

- 320 A diamonds
  Cut twenty 1¾-inch strips for strip sets.

From Fabric #6 (blue-and-black print)), cut:

- 192 A diamonds
  Cut twelve 1¾-inch strips for strip sets.

- 32 B diamonds

- Eighteen 1½-inch border strips

- Reserve the remaining fabric for binding

Fabric Key

Fabric #1   Yellow solid

Fabric #2   Blue-and-yellow print

Fabric #3   Brown paisley stripe

Fabric #4   Gold print

Fabric #5   Dark blue and medium blue print

Fabric #6   Blue-and-black print

Making the Small Corner Stars

1. Referring to the **Fabric Key** and **Diagram 1** for placement, sew a Fabric #3 B diamond to a Fabric #6 B diamond. Sew a Fabric #2 B diamond to a Fabric #3 B diamond. Press the seam allowances toward the paisley diamonds. Join the two sets of diamonds to form a large pieced diamond. Press the seam allowance to one side. Repeat to make a total of 32 pieced diamonds.

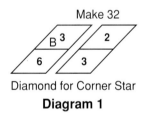

Make 32

Diamond for Corner Star
Diagram 1

2. As you join the pieces for the stars, do not sew into the seam allowances at the beginning and end of the seams. Backstitch to secure the ends of seams. See **Diagram 2.** Leaving the seam allowances unsewn will enable you to set the squares and triangles into the outside of the stars. It will also allow for easier pressing where all diamond points come together in the center. With the small blue-and-yellow print diamonds toward the center, sew four pieced diamonds into a half star as shown in **Diagram 3.** Repeat to make a total of eight half stars.

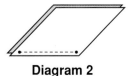

Diagram 2

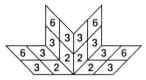

Half Star for Corner Block
Diagram 3

3. To make one star, join two half stars matching seam intersections and points. Press seams to one side so they radiate around the star. Repeat to make a total of four stars.

4. To complete the star block, refer to **Diagram 4.** Set a C triangle into alternate openings around the star as shown. Then, set a D square into the remaining four openings. Refer to "Setting-In Pieces" on page 155 for details. Press seam allowances toward the triangles and squares. Repeat to make a total of four star blocks.

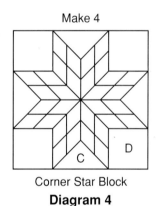

Make 4

Corner Star Block
Diagram 4

Making the Large Pieced Diamonds

Diagram 5 shows one large pieced diamond. The numbers on the small diamonds correspond with the fabric numbers. The rows of small diamonds are indicated by heavy lines and labeled by letter. To quick-piece the large diamonds, make strip sets, cut rows of joined small diamonds from them, and then join the rows. Refer to Steps 1 through 5 that follow for quick-piecing the diamonds.

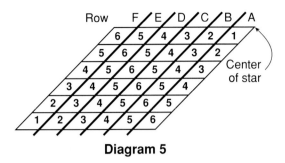

Row F E D C B A

Center of star

Diagram 5

1. Sew together 1¾-inch strips. As you join the strips, stagger the ends by approximately 1¾ inches as shown in **Diagram 6.** To make the strip set for Row A, sew strips together in the following order: 1, 2, 3, 4, 5, 6. Press the seam allowances away from the top (#1) strip. Make two of these strip sets.

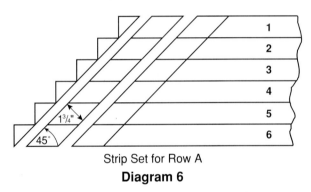

Strip Set for Row A

Diagram 6

2. Use a rotary cutter and a ruler with a 45 degree angle line to cut the strip set. Place the ruler so the 45 degree angle line is parallel to the seam lines. Cut rows of diamonds, each measuring 1¾ inches wide. Cut 16 rows of diamonds from each Strip Set A.

3. In a similar manner, make two each of strip sets B, C, D, E, and F and cut 16 rows of diamonds from each strip set. Sew fabric strips together in the following order:

Strip Set B: 2, 3, 4, 5, 6, 5
Strip Set C: 3, 4, 5, 6, 5, 4
Strip Set D: 4, 5, 6, 5, 4, 3
Strip Set E: 5, 6, 5, 4, 3, 2
Strip Set F: 6, 5, 4, 3, 2, 1

4. Use six rows of diamonds, one row from each type of strip set to make a large diamond. Lay out the rows as shown in **Diagram 5.** Join the rows, matching seam intersections and diamond points. Press the seams to one side.

Tip: *Take care not to stretch the bias edges of the diamonds when pressing. By pressing down on the seams and not sliding your iron from side to side, you can avoid stretching your diamonds out of shape.* ★

5. Repeat to make 32 large diamonds.

Assembling the Quilt Top

As you assemble the pieces for the star, do not sew into the seam allowances at the beginning and end of seams. Leaving the seam allowances free will enable you to set in the successive pieces. Backstitch to secure each end of the seams.

Making the Center Star

1. With the small yellow diamonds toward the center, sew two pairs of large diamonds together, then join the pairs to create a half star, as shown in **Diagram 7.** Make another half star with four more diamonds.

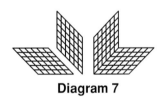

Diagram 7

2. Sew the two half stars together. Press seams to one side so they radiate around the star.

3. Set a large yellow F square into each opening around the star, as shown in **Diagram 8.** Refer to "Setting-In Pieces" on page 155 for details.

F

Diagram 8

Making the Broken Star

Refer to **Diagram 9** for Steps 1 through 4.

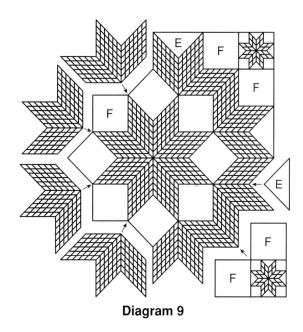

Diagram 9

1. Join a set of three large diamonds with yellow diamonds meeting at the tip. Make eight sets of three diamonds.

2. Set a group of three diamonds into the opening between squares on the center star. Press the seam allowances toward the squares. Repeat, adding all sets of three diamonds to the quilt center.

3. Set two F squares and one corner star into the opening at the corner of the outer star. Press the seam allowances toward the squares. Repeat to complete all four corners.

4. Set the E triangles into the openings along the sides of the outer star. Press the seam allowances toward the triangles.

Making and Adding the Borders

1. To piece the narrow borders, divide two of the blue border strips into four equal length pieces. Sew two full-length blue border strips and one quarter strip together to make a longer border. Repeat to make a total of eight borders.

2. Center and sew a narrow border to each long side of each brown paisley border. Press seam allowances toward the paisley fabric.

3. Referring to the **Quilt Diagram,** sew the borders to the quilt top. Your border strips will be longer than your quilt length. *Do not cut off excess fabric.* The extra length will be needed to miter the corners of the borders. Press the seam allowances toward the borders. Miter the border corner seams, referring to page 160 for more detailed directions.

Quilting and Finishing

1. Mark desired quilting designs onto the quilt top. The quilt pictured has outline quilting around each diamond, and quilting in the borders follows the paisley design of the border fabric. Feathered arcs are quilted in the large yellow squares and triangles.

2. To piece the quilt back, divide the backing fabric into three 2½-yard pieces. Join the three panels along their long edges. Press the seam allowances toward the outer panels.

3. Layer the quilt back, batting, and quilt top; baste. Trim the quilt back and batting so they are approximately 3 inches larger than the quilt top on all sides.

4. Quilt all marked designs and add any other quilting such as outline quilting, as desired.

5. From the blue-and-black print fabric, make approximately 360 inches of French-fold binding. See page 164 for suggested binding widths and instructions on making and attaching binding.

6. Sew the binding to the quilt. Trim excess batting and backing, and hand finish binding to the wrong side of the quilt.

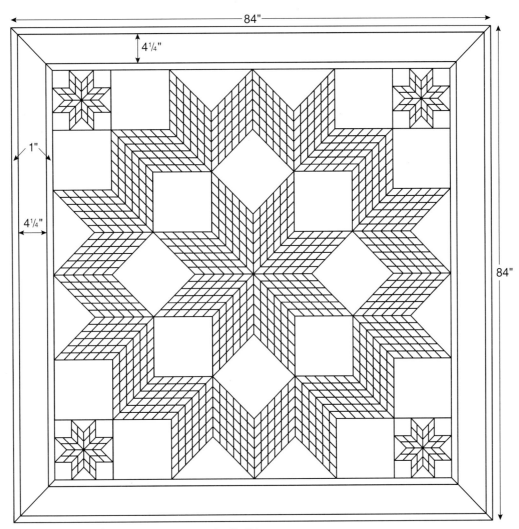

Quilt Diagram

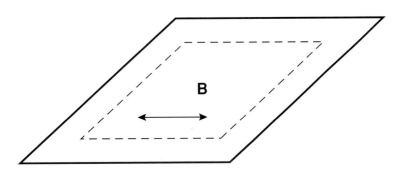

Fantasy Remembered

Quiltmaker: Joyce Stewart

This quilt began with the bright print Hoffman Challenge fabric. Joyce, who has a passion for color, played with many fabric possibilities before deciding to mix the vibrant shades in the challenge fabric with pastel versions of the same colors. And what better choice of blocks to use for all these colors than Joseph's Coat? To finish off this splendid wallhanging, Joyce added Celtic appliqué in the border and ended up winning a first place ribbon in the 1992-93 Hoffman Challenge.

Skill Level: Intermediate

Size: Finished quilt is 39 inches square
Finished star block is 12 inches square

Fabrics and Supplies

✓ 1½ yards of tan print fabric for borders, patchwork, and binding

✓ ½ yard of medium pink print fabric for patchwork and border appliqué

✓ ½ yard of pastel floral print for patchwork and border insets

✓ ⅓ yard *each* of dark blue, light pink, and bright multicolored print fabrics for patchwork

✓ ⅛ yard of fuchsia print fabric for patchwork

✓ ⅛ yard, or scraps, of light blue print fabric for patchwork

✓ 1¼ yards of fabric for quilt back

✓ Crib-size quilt batting (45 × 60 inches)

✓ Rotary cutter, ruler, and mat

✓ Template plastic

✓ Tracing paper

✓ Black permanent marker

✓ ⅜-inch-wide Celtic or bias bar (optional)

Cutting

All measurements include ¼-inch seam allowances. Measurements for the outer borders are longer than the quilt dimensions. *Do not trim off the extra fabric;* it will be used to miter the border corners. The instructions are written for quick-cutting the A, B, C, D, E, F, and G pieces using a rotary cutter and a ruler. Cut all strips across the fabric. For some of the pieces, the quick-cutting method will result in leftover fabric.

Make templates for appliqué pieces X and Y from the patterns on page 83. The appliqué patterns are finished size; add seam allowances when cutting out fabric. Instructions for making and using templates are on page 153.

You may want to cut just enough pieces to make one block to test your cutting and seam allowances for accuracy. If your finished block does not measure the size stated above, you can make adjustments before cutting all your fabric.

From the tan print fabric, cut:

• Four 6½-inch border strips

• 8 A squares and 4 F rectangles
Cut one 2-inch strip. From the strip cut eight 2-inch squares and four 2 × 6½-inch rectangles.

• 32 C triangles
Cut two 3⅞-inch strips. From the strips cut sixteen 3⅞-inch squares. Cut each square in half diagonally to make two triangles.

• 36 D triangles
Cut one 4¼-inch strip. From the strip cut nine 4¼-inch squares. Cut each square in half diagonally in both directions to make four triangles.

• Reserve the remaining fabric for binding

From the medium pink print fabric, cut:

• 4 E squares
Cut one 3½-inch strip. From the strip cut four 3½-inch squares.

• 32 B triangles
Cut one 2⅜-inch strip. From the strip cut sixteen 2⅜-inch squares. Cut each square in half diagonally to make two triangles.

• Reserve the remaining fabric for border appliqué

From the pastel floral print fabric, cut:

• 48 A squares
Cut three 2-inch strips. From the strips cut forty-eight 2-inch squares.

• 24 G squares
Cut two 2⅝-inch strips. From the strips cut twenty-four 2⅝-inch squares.

• 8 X pieces

• 4 Y pieces

From the dark blue print fabric, cut:

• 80 B triangles
Cut three 2⅜-inch strips. From the strips cut forty 2⅜-inch squares. Cut each square in half diagonally to make two triangles.

From the light pink print fabric, cut:

• 56 B triangles
Cut two 2⅜-inch strips. From the strips cut twenty-eight 2⅜-inch squares. Cut each

square in half diagonally to make two triangles.

From the multicolored print fabric, cut:
• Four 1-inch border strips
• 9 E squares
  Cut one 3½-inch strip. From the strip cut nine 3½-inch squares.

From the fuchsia print fabric, cut:
• 32 B triangles
  Cut one 2⅜-inch strip. From the strip cut sixteen 2⅜-inch squares. Cut each square in half diagonally to make two triangles.

From the light blue print fabric, cut:
• 32 B triangles
  Cut one 2⅜-inch strip. From the strip cut sixteen 2⅜-inch squares. Cut each square in half diagonally to make two triangles.

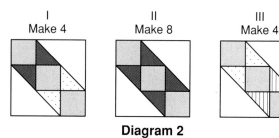

Piecing for I, II, III Units
Diagram 1

I
Make 4

II
Make 8

III
Make 4

Diagram 2

Piecing the Patchwork Units

The quilt is made from a combination of large squares and two types of pieced units. These units are pieced in a variety of color combinations, which are labeled with Roman numerals I through VIII.

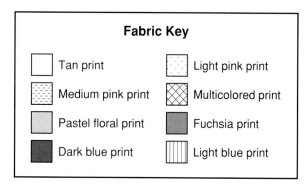

Fabric Key

Tan print

Medium pink print

Pastel floral print

Dark blue print

Light pink print

Multicolored print

Fuchsia print

Light blue print

Piecing the I, II, and III Units
All of the I, II, and III units are pieced in the same manner, as shown in **Diagram 1**. You will need to refer to the **Fabric Key** and **Diagram 2** for the number of units to make in each color variation (I, II, and III) and for fabric placement within each variation.

1. To make a I unit, lay out the pieces required as shown in **Diagram 2**. Then, referring to **Diagram 1**, sew the B triangles to the sides of the A squares as shown. Press seam allowances toward the squares. Join the three A/B units to make a center unit. Sew a C triangle to opposite sides of the center unit as shown. Press seam allowances toward the C triangles. Repeat to make a total of four variation I units.

2. Make eight variation II and four variation III units, referring to **Diagram 2** for fabric placement. Piece each of these units in the same manner as you did for the I units.

Piecing the IV, V, VI, and VII Units
All of the IV, V, VI, and VII units are pieced as shown in **Diagram 3**. Refer to the **Fabric Key** and **Diagram 4** for the number of units to make in each color variation (IV, V, VI, and VII) and for fabric placement within each variation.

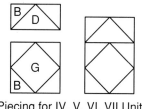

Piecing for IV, V, VI, VII Units
Diagram 3

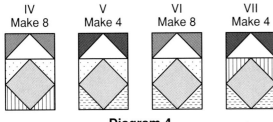

IV	V	VI	VII
Make 8	Make 4	Make 8	Make 4

Diagram 4

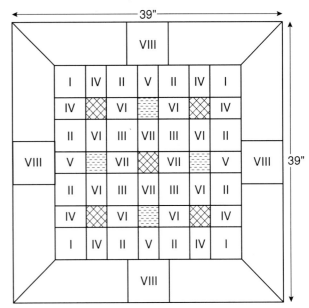

Quilt Assembly Diagram

1. To make a IV unit, lay out the pieces required as shown in **Diagram 4.** Referring to **Diagram 3,** make the top section by sewing a B triangle to the two short sides of a D triangle. Press seams toward the B triangles. To make the lower section, sew a B triangle to two opposite sides of a G square. Press the seam allowances toward the B triangles. Sew B triangles to the remaining two sides of the square and press seams toward the triangles. Sew the two sections together. Press the seam allowance toward the D triangle.

2. Make eight of variation IV, four of variation V, eight of variation VI, and four of variation VII, referring to **Diagram 4** for fabric placement.

Assembling the Inner Quilt Top

1. Referring to the **Quilt Assembly Diagram** and the **Fabric Key,** lay out the seven types of units and the E squares (as shown on the diagram).

2. Sew the units and squares together in seven horizontal rows. Press seam allowances in opposite directions from row to row.

3. Join the rows. Press the seam allowances to one side.

Making and Adding the Borders

1. Referring to **Diagram 5** and the **Fabric Key,** lay out the pieces for one VIII unit. Sew a B triangle to both short sides of the three D triangles. Press seam allowances away from the D triangles. Make three D/B units for each VIII block. Sew a D/B unit to two opposite sides of the E square. Press seams toward the E square.

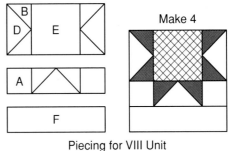

Make 4

Piecing for VIII Unit
Diagram 5

2. Sew an A square to both short sides of the remaining D/B unit as shown. Press the seam allowances toward the squares.

3. Referring to **Diagram 5,** join the three rows. Press seam allowances toward the F rectangle. Repeat to make a total of four variation VIII units.

4. To make the four borders for the quilt sides, cut each 6½-inch tan border strip in half to make eight short border sections.

5. Sew a tan border section to opposite sides of each VIII unit as shown in **Diagram 6** on page 82. Press seam allowances toward the tan fabric.

Border   VIII   Border

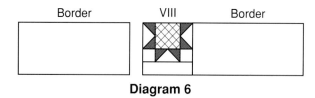

Diagram 6

6. Cut each 1-inch multicolored border strip in half to make a total of eight strips. Press under ¼ inch along one long side of each strip.

7. Referring to **Diagram 7,** appliqué a multi-colored strip to the top edge of each tan border section, aligning the top raw edges of the multi-colored strips with the top raw edges of the tan borders. Angle the narrow strips along the edges of the stars within the VIII units and appliqué.

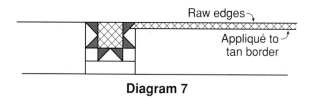

Raw edges

Appliqué to tan border

Diagram 7

8. Sew the borders to the quilt top. Your border strips will be longer than your quilt length. *Do not cut off excess fabric.* The extra length will be needed to miter the corners of the borders. Press the seam allowances toward the borders. Miter the border corner seams, refer-ring to page 160 for more detailed directions.

9. Using the **Border Appliqué Patterns I** and **II** and referring to the **Border Placement Diagram,** transfer placement guides onto the borders. To transfer guides, trace the border appliqué patterns on tracing paper. Darken the lines with a black permanent marker. Lay your tracing paper guide underneath your border fab-ric, and trace the design lightly on your fabric with a pencil.

10. Following the instructions with your bias bars or those in "Making Bias Strips for Stems and Vines" on page 158, cut and prepare approximately 260 inches of medium pink bias to finish ⅜ inch wide for the border appliqué. Or, if you don't have bias bars, see "Make Your Own Bias Guide" on the opposite page.

Border Placement Diagram

11. Pin or baste the X and Y appliqué pieces in position on the borders. Baste bias along the placement outlines. Appliqué bias in place, stitch-ing through the X and Y pieces to secure them.

Quilting and Finishing

1. Mark quilting designs onto the quilt top. The border on the quilt shown is quilted with ½-inch diagonal cross-hatching inside of the bias trim. The outer portion of the border is quilted in diagonal lines ½ inch apart. Some patchwork pieces are outline quilted in the ditch; others are quilted ¼ inch from seams.

2. Layer the quilt back, batting, and quilt top; baste. Trim the quilt back and batting so they are approximately 3 inches larger than the quilt top on all sides.

3. Quilt all marked designs.

4. Make approximately 170 inches of French-fold binding from the remaining tan print fabric. See page 164 for instructions on making and attaching binding.

5. Sew the binding to the quilt top. Trim the excess batting and backing, and hand finish the binding on the wrong side of the quilt. Refer to page 167 for adding a hanging sleeve.

Match with Pattern II

MAKE YOUR OWN BIAS GUIDE

Using a metal or plastic bias bar helps to speed up the process of making narrow bias strips. It also helps assure that your bias strips all have a consistent width. These bars are available commercially, and directions for using them can be found on page 158 under "Making Bias Strips for Stems and Vines."

You can also make your own bias guide easily from lightweight cardboard or poster board. To make a guide, cut a strip from the cardboard equal to the finished width of your bias strips. For more accurate cutting, use a rotary cutter in which you've placed an old blade (one that you don't want to use on fabric anymore). Lay the cardboard on your cutting mat, measure the width strip you need with your rotary ruler, and cut the cardboard strip as you would a strip of fabric.

Because a homemade cardboard bias guide won't slide along your fabric quite as easily as a metal or plastic one, the recommended technique for using it is a bit different. Center the bar on the wrong side of your fabric strip, and using the tip of your iron, fold one raw edge of the strip over the bar. Repeat with the other raw edge. Remove the bias bar, and press the strip one more time. ♦

X

One-half of Y

Align with corner seam on mitered border

Patterns are finished size. Add seam allowances when cutting pieces from fabric.

One-half of Border Appliqué Pattern I

Match with center of border strip

**One-half of Border
Appliqué Pattern II**

Match with Pattern I

Shaded area indicates overlap of Patterns I and II

Moon and Stars

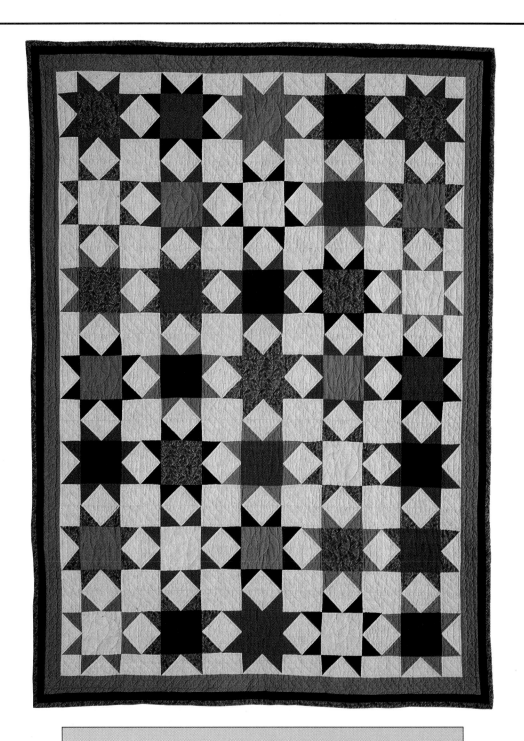

Quiltmaker: Sara Hedrick

In her very first quilting project, Sara turned five fabrics into 19 different Variable Star combinations to make this charming lap quilt. Her secret? Selecting fabrics with high contrast and tying them all together with a lovely coordinating print fabric. To complete this celestial celebration, a crescent moon and star are quilted in the center of each block.

Skill Level: Easy

Size: Finished quilt is 56 × 76 inches
Finished block is 10 inches square

Fabrics and Supplies

✓ 2¼ yards of cream solid fabric for patchwork

✓ 1¼ yards of paisley print fabric for patch-work and binding

✓ 1 yard of navy solid fabric for outer bor-der and patchwork

✓ 1¼ yards of medium teal solid fabric for inner border and patchwork

✓ ¾ yard of fuchsia print fabric for patchwork

✓ 3½ yards of fabric for quilt back

✓ Twin-size quilt batting (72 × 90 inches)

✓ Rotary cutter, ruler, and mat

✓ Template plastic (optional)

Cutting

All measurements include a ¼-inch seam allowance. The measurements for the borders include several extra inches in length; trim them to the exact length before sewing them to the quilt top. Instructions given are for quick-cutting the pieces with a rotary cutter and ruler. Cut all strips across the fabric width.

You may want to cut just enough pieces to make one block to test your cutting and seam allowances for accuracy. If your finished block does not measure the size stated above, you can make adjustments before cutting all your fabric.

From the cream solid fabric, cut:
• 140 A triangles
  Cut six 6¼-inch strips. Cut the strips into 35 squares, each 6¼ inches square. Cut each square in half diagonally in both directions to make four triangles.

• 140 C squares
  Cut ten 3-inch strips. Cut the strips into 3-inch squares.

• 7 D squares
  Cut one 5½-inch strip. Cut the strip into 5½-inch squares.

From the paisley print fabric, cut:
• 7 D squares
  Cut one 5½-inch strip. Cut the strip into 5½-inch squares.

• 72 B triangles
  Cut three 3⅜-inch strips. Cut the strips into 36 squares, each 3⅜ inches square. Cut each square in half diagonally to make two triangles.

• Reserve the remaining fabric for binding

From the navy solid fabric, cut:
• Seven 1½-inch outer border strips

• 64 B triangles
  Cut three 3⅜-inch strips. Cut the strips into 32 squares, each 3⅜ inches square. Cut each square in half diagonally to make two triangles.

• 7 D squares
  Cut one 5½-inch strip. Cut the strip into 5½-inch squares.

From the medium teal solid fabric, cut:
• Seven 2½-inch inner border strips

• 7 D squares
  Cut one 5½-inch strip. Cut the strip into 5½-inch squares.

• 72 B triangles
  Cut three 3⅜-inch strips. Cut the strips into 36 squares, each 3⅜ inches square. Cut each square in half diagonally to make two triangles.

From the fuchsia print fabric, cut:
• 7 D squares
  Cut one 5½-inch strip. Cut the strip into 5½-inch squares.

• 72 B triangles
  Cut three 3⅜-inch strips. Cut the strips into 36 squares, each 3⅜ inches square. Cut each square in half diagonally to make two triangles.

Piecing the Star Blocks

1. Referring to the **Fabric Placement Chart**, lay out the pieces for one block. You will need four A triangles, four C squares, eight matching B triangles, and one D square.

2. Sew B triangles to the two short sides of an A triangle as shown in **Diagram 1.** Press seams toward the B triangles. You will have four of these units per block.

Diagram 1

3. Referring to **Diagram 2,** sew the A/B units to two opposite sides of a D square. Press seam allowances toward the square. Sew a C square to each end of two A/B units. Press seam allowances toward the C squares.

4. Join the three rows as shown in **Diagram 3.** Press seams away from the center square. Repeat to make 35 blocks. The numbers on the **Fabric Placement Chart** show the numbers of blocks made from each fabric combination.

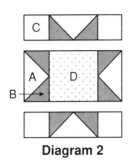

Diagram 2

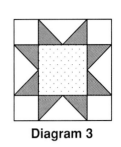

Diagram 3

Assembling the Quilt Top

1. Referring to the **Quilt Diagram** on page 88, join the blocks in seven horizontal rows with five blocks per row. Press seams in opposite directions from row to row.

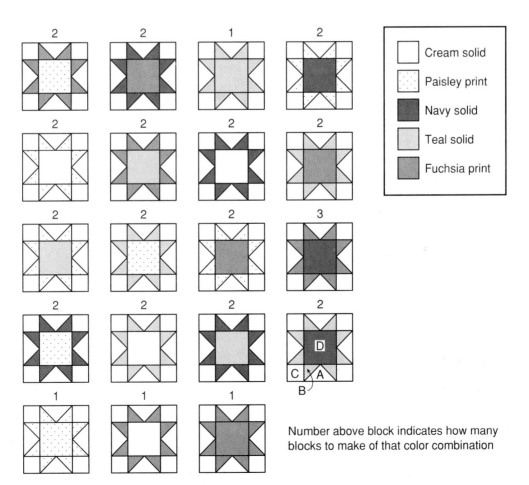

	Cream solid
	Paisley print
	Navy solid
	Teal solid
	Fuchsia print

Number above block indicates how many blocks to make of that color combination

Fabric Placement Chart

2. Join the rows, aligning the alternately pressed seams. The inner quilt top should measure $50\frac{1}{2} \times 70\frac{1}{2}$ inches, including seam allowances.

3. You will need to piece the four inner borders from the seven teal border strips. Join two strips with diagonal seams for each of the side borders. (See **Diagram 4.**) To make the top and bottom borders, cut one of the remaining teal strips in half. Sew a half strip to each of the two remaining full strips with diagonal seams.

4. Measure the length of the quilt through the center and trim the side borders to the correct length. Sew one border to each side of the quilt top. Press seams toward the borders.

Measure the width of the quilt through the center, including the side borders. Trim top and bottom borders to the correct length and sew them to the quilt. Press seams toward borders.

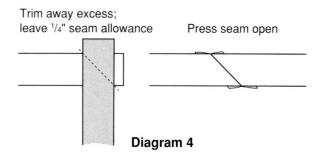

Trim away excess; leave 1/4" seam allowance   Press seam open

Diagram 4

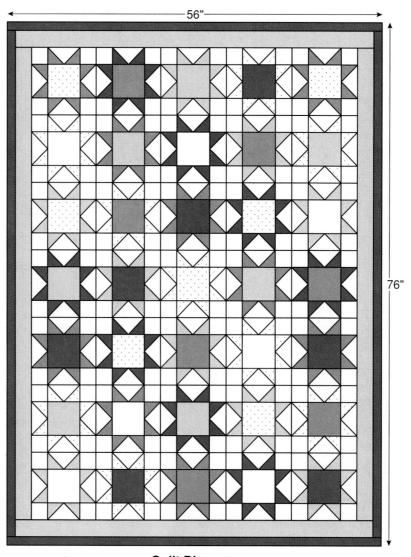

Quilt Diagram

5. Piece four outer borders from the navy border strips in the manner described for the teal borders in Step 3 above. Trim and sew the outer borders to the quilt top in the manner described in Step 4 above.

Quilting and Finishing

1. Mark quilting designs. Patterns for the moon and star motifs used in the D squares as well as the rope design used in the teal borders are on this page. The quilt shown also has outline quilting ¼ inch from the patchwork seams, plus diagonal and straight lines quilted in the solid cream areas.

2. Cut the backing fabric into two equal lengths and trim away the selvages. Sew the two pieces together along the long edges. Press seam allowances in one direction. The seam will run parallel to the short sides of the quilt.

3. Layer the backing, batting, and quilt top; baste. Trim the backing and batting so they are approximately 3 inches larger than the quilt top.

4. Quilt all marked designs.

5. From the paisley fabric, make approximately 280 inches of French-fold binding. See page 164 for making and attaching binding.

6. Sew the binding to the quilt top. Trim the excess batting and backing, and hand finish the binding on the wrong side of the quilt.

Moon and Star Quilting Design

Border Quilting Design

Old Schoolhouse

Quiltmaker: Norma Grasse

Traditional schoolhouse blocks pieced in many different antique black prints are brought to life with red-and-white striped sashing stars. The background fabric is a reproduction of a shirting print that was popular around the turn of the century. Folksy six-pointed star flowers with doughnut holes twinkle between two rows of sawtooth borders to frame the quilt. Norma's decision to include a sprinkling of yellow stars among the black and red ones adds the final touch of whimsy to this delightful quilt.

Skill Level: Intermediate

Size: Finished quilt is 75 inches square
Finished block is 9 inches square

Fabrics and Supplies

✓ 5 yards of off-white shirting fabric with black print for borders, houses, sawtooth borders, and sashing strips

✓ 1½ yards of black solid fabric for sawtooth borders and binding

✓ ⅔ yard *each* of red-and-white stripe fabric and red-and-white print fabric for sashing squares and triangles

✓ ½ yard of dark red print fabric for chimneys, border star flowers, and doors

✓ ⅓ yard of white-and-red plaid fabric for windows

✓ Fat quarters (18 × 22-inch rectangles), or scraps, *each* of 25 black print fabrics for houses and border star flowers

✓ Fat quarters (18 × 22-inch rectangles), or scraps, of yellow print for border star flowers

✓ 4½ yards of fabric for quilt back

✓ Full-size quilt batting (81 × 96 inches)

✓ Rotary cutter, ruler, and mat

✓ Template plastic

Cutting

All measurements include ¼-inch seam allowances. Measurements for the borders are longer than needed; trim them to the exact length before adding them to the quilt top.

Instructions given are for quick-cutting pieces A through H, X, and Y using a rotary cutter and a ruler. Cut all strips across the fabric unless directed otherwise. Note that for some of the pieces, the quick-cutting method will result in leftover fabric. For the remaining pieces, I through O, V, W, and Z, make templates from the patterns on pages 96–97. Instructions for making and using templates are on page 153. Turn templates over to cut reverse I, O, and W pieces.

You may want to cut just enough pieces to make one block to test your templates, cutting, and seam allowances for accuracy. If your finished block does not measure the size stated above, you can make adjustments before cutting all your fabric.

From the off-white fabric, cut one 74-inch-long piece. From this piece, cut:
• Four 6½ × 74-inch *lengthwise* borders
• 25 *each* of K, M, O, and O reverse pieces for schoolhouse blocks

From the remaining off-white fabric, cut:
• 25 rectangles for the top row of the blocks
  Cut seven 1½-inch strips. From these strips cut 25 rectangles, each 1½ × 9½ inches.
• 25 D house rectangles
  Cut four 1-inch strips. From these strips cut 25 rectangles, each 1 × 5 inches.
• 344 Y sawtooth triangles
  Cut eleven 2⅜-inch strips. From the strips cut 172 squares, each 2⅜ inches square. Cut each square in half diagonally to make two triangles.
• 60 V sashing strips
• One 3½-inch strip for the chimney strip set
• Two 2½-inch strips for the chimney strip set

From the black solid fabric, cut:
• 344 Y sawtooth triangles
  Cut eleven 2⅜-inch strips. From the strips cut 172 squares, each 2⅜ inches square. Cut each square in half diagonally to make two triangles.
• Reserve the remaining fabric for binding

From the red-and-white stripe fabric and the red-and-white print fabric, cut a total of:
• 36 X sashing squares
  Cut three 2½-inch strips. From the strips cut 36 squares, each 2½ inches square.
• 120 W and 120 W reverse triangles for sashing strips

From the dark red print fabric, cut:
• Two 1½-inch strips for the chimney strip set
• 4 Z border star flowers
• 25 A doors
  Cut three 1½-inch strips. Cut the strips into 25 rectangles, each 1½ × 4 inches. Note: One

of the doors on the quilt shown was cut from black stripe fabric, rather than from red print.

From the white-and-red plaid fabric, cut:

- 25 H squares for house peak windows
  Cut one 1½-inch strip. From this strip cut 25 squares, each 1½ inches square.
- 50 F windows
  Cut four 1½-inch strips. From the strips cut 50 rectangles, each 1½ × 3 inches.

From each of the 25 black print fabrics, cut:

- One I, I reverse, J, L, and N piece
- One 1½ × 22-inch strip
    ### From this strip, cut:
    - One 4½-inch C rectangle
    - One 3-inch F rectangle
    - Two 5-inch G rectangles
- Two 2 × 4-inch B rectangles
- Two 1¼ × 3-inch E rectangles

From the remaining black print fabrics, cut:

- 36 Z border star flowers

From the yellow print fabric, cut:

- 4 Z border star flowers

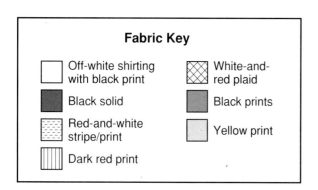

Fabric Key

☐ Off-white shirting with black print	▨ White-and-red plaid
■ Black solid	▨ Black prints
▨ Red-and-white stripe/print	☐ Yellow print
▥ Dark red print	

Piecing the Blocks

Each block is assembled in four rows: chimney (row 3), roof (row 2), and bottom of the house (row 1). Row 4 is simply a strip of background fabric added to the top of the block. See **Block Diagram.**

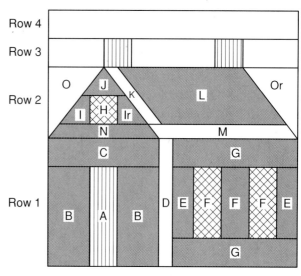

Block Diagram

Making the Chimney Sections

1. Referring to the **Fabric Key** and **Diagram 1,** sew a 1½-inch dark red print strip to the long sides of a 3½-inch off-white strip. Sew a 2½-inch off-white strip to the remaining long side of each red strip. Press the seam allowances toward the red strips.

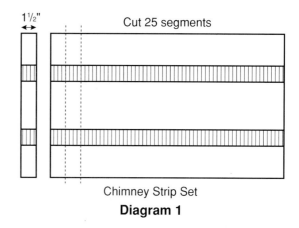

Chimney Strip Set
Diagram 1

2. Cut the chimney strip set into 25 segments, each 1½ inches wide.

Assembling the Schoolhouse Blocks

Refer to the **Block Diagram** to piece 25 Schoolhouse blocks. Make sure that all black pieces for a single block are from the same black print fabric.

1. To make the house front, sew a black print B rectangle to the long sides of a dark red A door piece. Press seam allowances toward the B pieces. Sew a black print C rectangle to the top edge of the door unit to complete the house front. See **Diagram 2.**

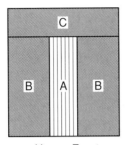

House Front

Diagram 2

2. To make the house side, sew a white-and-red plaid F window rectangle to each long edge of a black print F rectangle. Add a black print E rectangle to the remaining long edge of the plaid rectangles. See **Diagram 3.** Press seam allowances away from the F windows. Sew a black print G rectangle to the top and bottom edges of the house side to complete the house side unit.

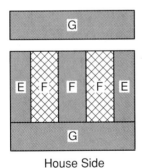

House Side

Diagram 3

3. To complete Row 1 of the block, sew an off-white D rectangle to the right side of the house front unit. Sew the house side unit to the opposite side of the D rectangle. Press the seam allowances away from the D rectangle. See **Diagram 4.**

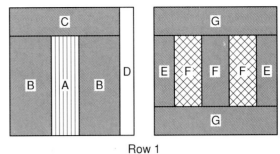

Row 1

Diagram 4

4. To make the house peak, sew black print I and I reverse pieces to opposite sides of a white-and-red plaid H window square. Press seam allowances away from the window. Sew a black print J triangle to the top edge of the H/I unit and a black print N piece to the bottom edge. Press seam allowances away from the H/I unit. See **Diagram 5.** Sew an off-white O triangle to the left side of the house peak. Press the seam allowances toward the O piece.

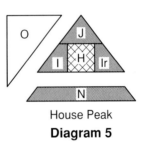

House Peak

Diagram 5

5. To complete the roof section, sew an off-white K piece to the left slanted edge of a black print L roof piece, as in **Diagram 6.** Press the seam allowance toward the roof. Sew an off-white M piece to the lower edge of the K/L unit. Press seam allowances toward M. Add an off-white O reverse triangle to the right slanted edge of the L roof piece. Press seam allowances toward O reverse.

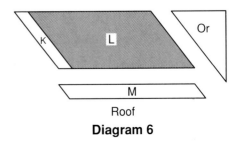

Roof

Diagram 6

6. Join the house peak and roof sections by sewing the long edge of piece K to the diagonal edge of the house peak unit to make Row 2.

7. Join Rows 1 and 2, being careful to match the roof peak seam intersections with those of the house front. See the **Block Diagram.**

8. Sew a chimney segment to the top edge of the house. Press seam allowances toward the chimney segment.

9. Sew a 1½ × 9½-inch off-white piece to the top edge of the chimney segment to complete the block. Your block should measure 9½ inches square, including seam allowances.

10. Repeat to make a total of 25 School-house blocks, each using a different black print fabric.

Assembling the Quilt Top

1. To piece one sashing strip, sew a red-and-white stripe or print W and W reverse triangle to each slanted end of an off-white V sashing strip

as shown in **Diagram 7.** Press the seam allowances toward the W pieces. Make 60 sashing strips.

Make 60

Sashing Strip
Diagram 7

2. Referring to the **Quilt Assembly Diagram,** sew the Schoolhouse blocks together in five horizontal rows with five blocks and six sashing strips in each row. Press seam allowances toward the blocks.

3. Make six horizontal sashing rows with six red-and-white stripe or print X sashing squares and five sashing strips in each row. Press the seam allowances toward the sashing squares.

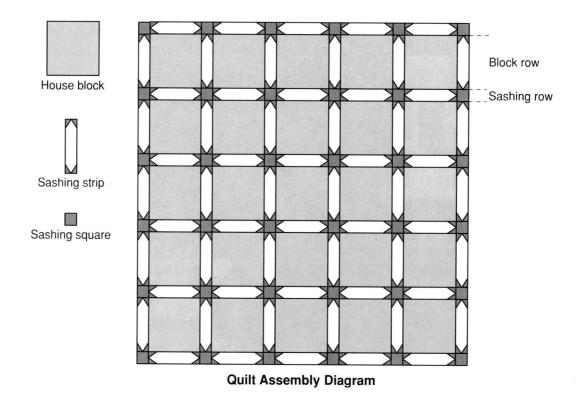

House block

Sashing strip

Sashing square

Block row

Sashing row

Quilt Assembly Diagram

4. Join the rows, beginning with a sashing row and alternating types of rows. Press the seam allowances to one side.

Adding the Borders

1. Sew an off-white Y triangle to a black solid Y triangle along their long diagonal edges to form a triangle-square, as shown in **Diagram 8.** Press the seam allowance toward the black triangle. Repeat to make a total of 344 black and off-white triangle-squares.

Triangle-Square
Diagram 8

2. Referring to the photo on page 90 for the direction of the slant of triangle-square seams, make sawtooth borders. Join 37 triangle-square units for the inner top and bottom borders. Join 39 triangle-square units for the inner side borders. Join 47 triangle-square units for the outer top and bottom borders, and 49 triangle-square units for the outer side borders. Press seam allowances to one side.

3. Sew the 37-unit sawtooth borders to the top and bottom edges of the quilt top. Sew the 39-unit sawtooth borders to the sides of the quilt top. Press seam allowances toward the quilt top.

4. Trim two off-white border strips to 60½ inches. This should be the width of your quilt. Sew the off-white borders to the top and bottom edges of the quilt, easing either the quilt or the borders to fit if necessary. Press seam allowances toward the off-white borders.

5. Trim two off-white border strips to 72½ inches. Sew the borders to the sides of the quilt top, easing to fit if necessary. Press seam allowances toward the off-white borders.

6. Sew the 47-unit sawtooth borders to the top and bottom of the quilt. Sew the 49-unit sawtooth borders to the sides of the quilt top. Press seam allowances toward the off-white borders.

7. Prepare the Z star flowers for appliqué. Instructions for appliqué are on page 156. Pin a star flower at each corner of the off-white border. Then pin ten star flowers along each border evenly spaced between the corner star flowers. Appliqué the star flowers in place.

Tip: *It is easier to appliqué if you do not cut out the center circle until after you have appliquéd the star flower to your border. When cutting out the circle, be sure to add a scant ¼-inch seam allowance to the inside edge of the circle.* ★

Quilting and Finishing

1. Mark desired quilting designs. The border is quilted with a diagonal grid of 1-inch squares, and the houses are outline quilted and filled in with parallel line quilting.

2. To piece the quilt back, cut the backing fabric into two 2¼-yard pieces. Cut one piece in half lengthwise. Sew a half panel to each long side of the full panel. Press the seam allowances toward the outer panels.

3. Layer the quilt back, batting, and quilt top; baste. Trim the quilt back and batting so they are approximately 3 inches larger than the quilt top on all sides.

4. Quilt all marked designs, and add additional quilting as desired.

5. Make approximately 320 inches of French-fold binding from the black solid fabric. See page 164 for instructions on making and attaching binding.

6. Sew the binding to the quilt. Trim the excess batting and backing, and hand finish the binding to the wrong side of the quilt. Refer to page 167 for instructions on making and attaching a hanging sleeve.

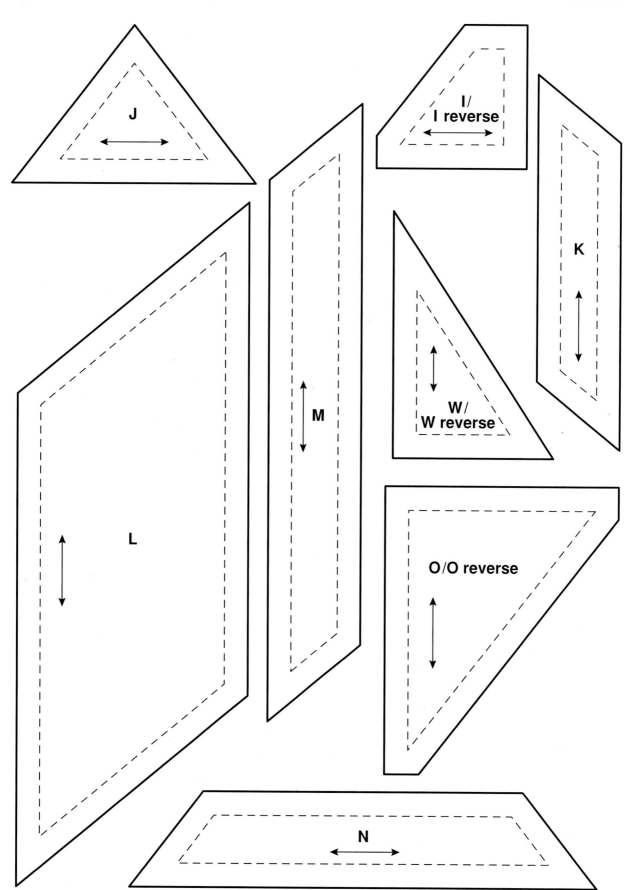

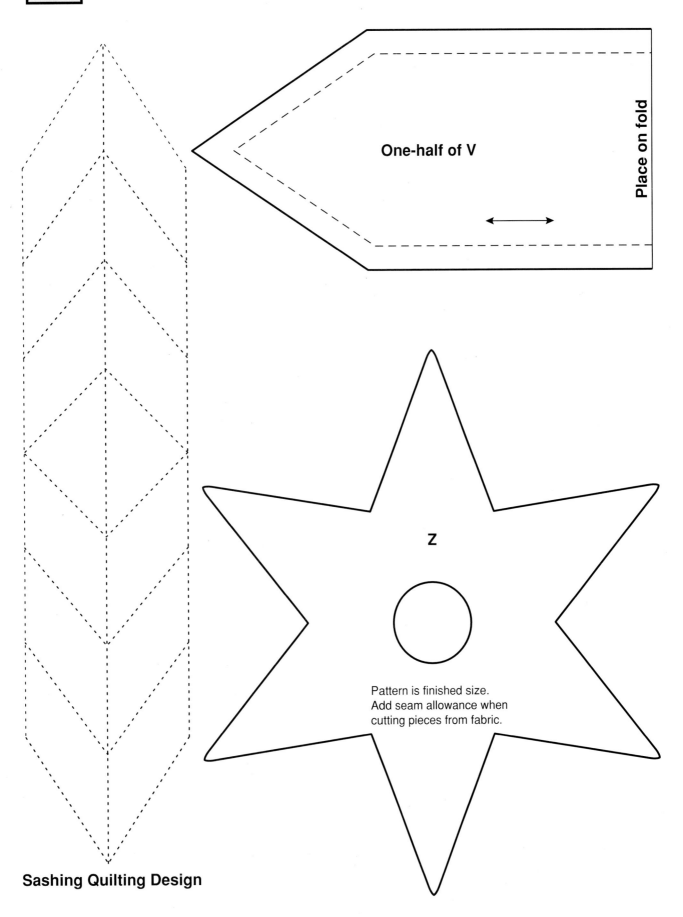

One-half of V

Place on fold

Z

Pattern is finished size.
Add seam allowance when
cutting pieces from fabric.

Sashing Quilting Design

Midnight Starburst

Quiltmaker: Carla Moore

When Carla decided to take up quilting, she asked her husband to help select fabrics for her first quilt, figuring if he liked the quilt he would become an enthusiastic supporter of her new interest. She never dreamed he'd choose yellow, orange, green, purple, and black solids! But when you see the vibrant stars of yellow and orange dancing across a black nighttime sky, and the partial stars of purple and green (which add depth to the design), there's no doubt Carla turned a color challenge into a winning quilt.

Skill Level: Intermediate

Size: Finished quilt is 77¼ × 85¼ inches
Finished block is 14 inches square (approximately 19¾ inches on the diagonal)

Fabrics and Supplies

- ✓ 6½ yards of black solid fabric for borders, triangles, patchwork, and binding
- ✓ 1 yard *each* of green solid and purple solid fabric for patchwork
- ✓ ½ yard *each* of yellow solid and orange solid fabric for patchwork
- ✓ 5¼ yards of fabric for quilt back
- ✓ Full-size quilt batting (81 × 96 inches)
- ✓ Rotary cutter, ruler, and mat
- ✓ Template plastic (optional)

Cutting

All measurements include ¼-inch seam allowances. The measurements for the borders include several extra inches in length; trim them to the exact length before sewing them to the quilt top.

The instructions are written for quick-cutting the pieces using a rotary cutter and a ruler. Cut all strips across the fabric width unless directed otherwise. Note that for some of the pieces, the quick-cutting method will result in leftover strips of fabric.

You may want to cut just enough pieces to make one block to test your cutting and seam allowances for accuracy. If your finished block does not measure the size stated above, you can make adjustments before cutting all your fabric.

From the black fabric, cut one 70-inch lengthwise piece. From this piece, cut:
- Two 9½ × 70-inch side borders cut *lengthwise*
- 8 setting triangles

Cut two 21-inch squares. Cut each square in half diagonally in both directions to make four triangles.
- 4 corner triangles
Cut two 10¾-inch squares. Cut each square in half diagonally to make two triangles.

From the black fabric, cut one 90-inch lengthwise piece. From this piece, cut:
- Two 13½ × 90-inch borders cut *lengthwise*
- 208 B squares
Cut six 2¼ × 90-inch *lengthwise* strips. From the strips, cut 208 squares, each 2¼ inches square.

From the black fabric, cut one 40-inch lengthwise piece. From this piece, cut:
- 416 A triangles
Cut fourteen 2⅝-inch crosswise strips. From these strips, cut 208 squares, each 2⅝ inches square. Cut each square in half diagonally to make two triangles.
- Reserve the remaining fabric for binding

From each of the green and purple fabrics, cut:
- 312 A triangles
Cut eleven 2⅝-inch strips. From these strips, cut 156 squares, each 2⅝ inches square. Cut each square in half diagonally to make two triangles.

From each of the yellow and orange fabrics, cut:
- 104 A triangles
Cut four 2⅝-inch strips. From these strips, cut 52 squares, each 2⅝ inches square. Cut each square in half diagonally to make two triangles.

Piecing the Starburst Blocks

As you piece the starburst blocks, plan your pressing strategy so that seams that will abut are pressed in opposite directions.

1. Referring to the **Fabric Key** and **Diagram 1** on page 100, lay out one starburst unit.

Fabric Key

☐ Black solid

▨ Green solid

◼ Purple solid

⬚ Yellow solid

▩ Orange solid

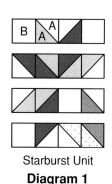

Starburst Unit
Diagram 1

Make 13

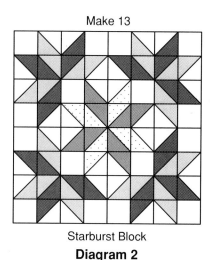

Starburst Block
Diagram 2

2. Sew pairs of A triangles together to form triangle-squares. Press the seam allowances toward the darker fabric. For each starburst unit, you need to make the following number of triangle-square color combinations:

purple/black = 3
purple/green = 3
green/black = 3
orange/black = 1
orange/yellow = 1
yellow/black = 1

You will also need four black squares for each starburst unit.

3. Join the triangle-squares and B squares to make four rows as shown in **Diagram 1.** Assemble the four rows to make one starburst unit. Repeat to make a total of 52 units.

4. Referring to **Diagram 2,** lay out four units as shown with the yellow and orange pieces at the block center. Join the top two units side to side and the bottom two units side to side. Press seams in opposite directions. Join the top and bottom units to make a starburst block. Repeat to make a total of 13 blocks.

Assembling the Quilt Top

1. Referring to the **Quilt Diagram,** lay out the blocks, setting triangles, and corner triangles as shown.

2. Sew the blocks together in diagonal rows, adding setting triangles to the ends as needed. The heavy lines on the diagram define the rows. Press the seam allowances in alternate directions from row to row. Join the rows. Add the corner triangles after the rows have been joined.

3. Measure the length of the quilt top through the center of the quilt (it should be approximately 59¾ inches). Trim the two 9½-inch borders to this length. Sew these borders to two opposite sides of the quilt top. Press the seam allowances toward the borders.

4. Measure the width of the quilt through the center, including the side borders (approximately 77¾ inches). Trim the two 13½-inch borders to this length. Sew the borders to the top and bottom edges of the quilt top. Press seam allowances toward the borders.

Quilting and Finishing

1. Mark quilting designs onto the quilt top. The quilt shown has ¼-inch outline quilting around the patchwork shapes, treating pairs of matching triangles that form diamond shapes as one unit. The setting triangles and borders are quilted with a diagonal grid of 1¾-inch squares.

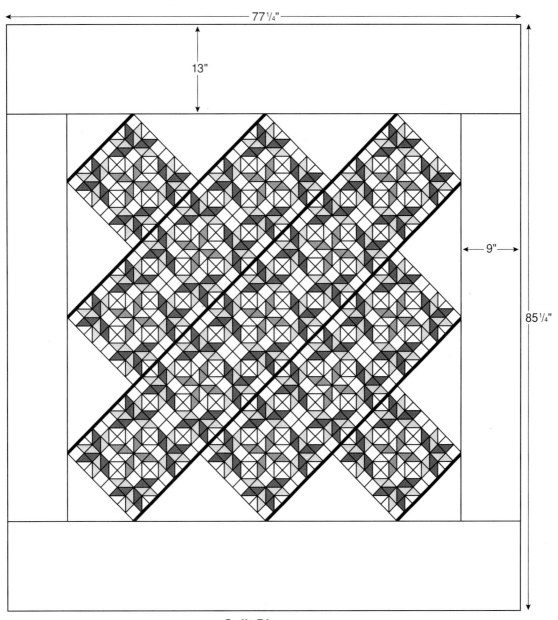

Quilt Diagram

2. To piece the quilt back, divide the backing fabric into two equal lengths. Divide one panel in half lengthwise. Sew a half panel to both long sides of the full panel. Press the seam allowances away from the center panel.

3. Layer the quilt back, batting, and quilt top; baste. Trim the quilt back and batting so they are approximately 3 inches larger than the quilt top on all sides.

4. Quilt all marked designs.

5. From the remaining black fabric, make approximately 340 inches of French-fold binding. See page 164 for suggested binding widths and instructions on making and attaching binding.

6. Sew the binding to the quilt. Trim excess batting and backing, and hand finish the binding on the wrong side of the quilt.

Hunter's Star Variation

Quiltmaker: Marilyn Michael

Marilyn designed her version of the Hunter's Star in response to
a quilt guild challenge to create a piece made entirely of right triangles. She cut hundreds of little triangles while working on the
design for this small quilt, but it was worth it. Her quilt not only
won first place in her guild challenge, it won ribbons in two
other shows. If you're looking for a way to use up some of those
scraps you've been collecting, this prize-winning quilt may be
the answer. And the quick-cutting techniques provided in the
directions will make using your scraps a snap.

Skill Level: Easy

Size: Finished quilt is 25 inches square
Finished block is 5 inches square

Fabrics and Supplies

✓ ⅝ yard total, or scraps, of various dark print fabrics for patchwork and border corner squares (Colors used in the quilt shown are blue, green, brown, and red.)

✓ ⅝ yard total, or scraps, of medium and light beige print fabrics for patchwork

✓ ⅛ yard of dark green print fabric for inner border

✓ ⅝ yard of dark blue print fabric for outer border and binding

✓ 1 yard of fabric for quilt back

✓ Quilt batting, at least 31 inches square

✓ Rotary cutter, ruler, and mat

✓ Template plastic (optional)

Cutting

All measurements include a ¼-inch seam allowance. The instructions are written for quick-cutting the pieces with a rotary cutter and ruler. Cut all strips across the fabric width.

You may want to cut just enough pieces to make one block to test your cutting and seam allowances for accuracy. If your finished block does not measure the size stated above, you can make adjustments before cutting all your fabric.

From the dark print fabrics, cut:
• 256 triangles
   Cut seven 2⅛-inch strips. From these strips, cut 128 squares, each 2⅛ inches square. Cut the squares in half diagonally to make two triangles.

• Four 1¼-inch border corner squares (Red was used in the quilt shown.)

From the beige print fabrics, cut:
• 256 triangles
   Cut seven 2⅛-inch strips. From these strips, cut 128 squares, each 2⅛ inches square. Cut the squares in half diagonally to make two triangles.

From the dark green print fabric, cut:
• Two 1¼-inch inner border strips

From the dark blue print fabric, cut:
• Four 2¼-inch outer border strips
• Reserve the remaining fabric for binding

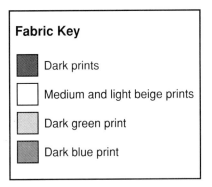

Fabric Key

Dark prints

Medium and light beige prints

Dark green print

Dark blue print

Piecing the Units

1. Referring to the **Fabric Key,** join dark print and beige print triangles as shown in **Diagram 1** to make 128 triangle-squares. Also make 64 triangle-squares using two dark print triangles and 64 using two beige print triangles. Press the seams toward the darker fabrics.

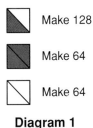

Make 128

Make 64

Make 64

Diagram 1

2. Lay out 16 triangle-squares in four horizontal rows of four triangle-squares per row, as shown in **Diagram 2,** to make a patchwork block. The stars in the quilt will form when these blocks are joined.

Tip: *If you want a star to be a particular color dark print, position triangle-squares of that color in one or both of the positions indicated by heavy lines in the diagram. Use this same color in four different* *blocks for each star. See the **Quilt Diagram** for positioning of the four blocks to form the star. The quilt shown features one red star, one brown star, and several blue stars.* ★

Make 16

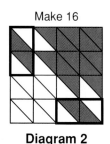

Diagram 2

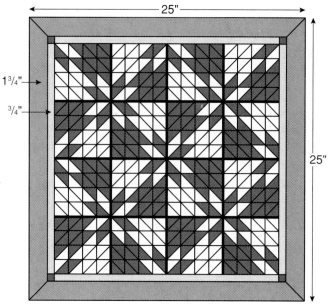

Quilt Diagram

3. Join the triangle-squares into rows. Press the seam allowances in opposite directions from row to row. Join the rows to complete a block. Repeat to make a total of 16 blocks.

Assembling the Quilt Top

1. Referring to the **Quilt Diagram,** lay out the 16 blocks in four horizontal rows with four blocks per row. The heavy lines on the diagram define the blocks. Be sure to position the blocks as shown in the diagram, and be careful in matching your star colors, if you have decided to make them specific colors.

2. Join the blocks into rows. Press the seam allowances in opposite directions from row to row. Join the rows.

3. Measure the length and width of the quilt top, measuring through the center of the quilt (the length and width should be the same). Cut the two green inner border strips in half to make four border strips. Trim the four strips to your length and width measurements.

4. Sew a border strip to two opposite sides of the quilt top. Press the seams toward the borders. Sew the border corner squares to the ends of the two remaining inner border strips. Sew these borders to the two remaining sides of the quilt. Press the seams toward the borders.

5. Sew the outer borders to the quilt top. Your border strips will be longer than your quilt length. *Do not cut off excess fabric.* The extra

length will be needed to miter the corners of the borders. Press the seam allowances toward the borders. Miter the border corner seams, referring to page 160 for more detailed directions.

Quilting and Finishing

1. Mark the quilt top. The quilt shown was hand quilted in the ditch along the diagonal seams of the patchwork, which don't need to be marked. The border is quilted with a three-tier swag pattern.

2. Layer the quilt back, batting, and quilt top; baste. Trim the quilt back and batting so they are approximately 3 inches larger than the quilt top on all sides.

3. Quilt as desired.

4. From the dark blue print fabric, make approximately 110 inches of French-fold binding. See page 164 for suggested binding widths and instructions on making and attaching binding.

5. Sew the binding to the quilt top. Trim the excess batting and backing, and hand finish the binding on the wrong side of the quilt. Refer to page 167 for adding a hanging sleeve.

Starburst

Quiltmaker: Diane Doro

Primary colors in dozens of prints, geometrics, plaids, and solids create a starburst effect similar to that seen through a kaleidoscope. Amazingly, this dramatic design is achieved by repeating just one patchwork block. It's the variety of prints and the position of the colors within each block that result in the stunning three-dimensional medallion look.

Skill Level: Intermediate

Size: Finished quilt is 34½ inches square
Finished block is 11½ inches square

Fabrics and Supplies

✓ ⅛ yard, or scraps, *each* of 3 different yellow fabrics

✓ ¼ yard *each* of 2 different yellow fabrics

✓ ⅛ yard, or scraps, *each* of 11 different red fabrics

✓ ⅛ yard, or scraps, *each* of 7 different medium or dark blue fabrics

✓ ¼ yard of 1 additional medium or dark blue fabric

✓ ⅓ yard of navy solid fabric for binding

✓ 1¼ yards of fabric for quilt back

✓ Crib-size quilt batting (45 × 60 inches)

✓ Template plastic

Cutting

All measurements include a ¼-inch seam allowance. Make templates for pieces A, B, C, D, and E from the patterns on pages 108–109. Instructions for making and using templates are on page 153. There are two types of D pieces in the quilt, D and D reverse (which is the mirror image of D). To cut D reverse pieces, simply flip the D template over.

You may want to cut just enough pieces to make one block to test your templates, cutting, and seam allowances for accuracy. If your finished block does not measure the size stated above, you can make adjustments before cutting all your fabric.

From the yellow #1 fabric (¼ yard), cut:
- 4 *each* of pieces B, D, D reverse, and E

From the yellow #2 fabric, cut:
- 4 *each* of pieces D and D reverse

From the yellow #3 fabric (¼ yard), cut:
- 9 A squares

From the yellow #4 fabric, cut:
- 8 B pieces

From the yellow #5 fabric, cut:
- 4 A squares
- 12 E triangles

From the red #1 fabric, cut:
- 8 C triangles

From the red #2 fabric, cut:
- 32 C triangles

From the red #3 fabric, cut:
- 12 B pieces

From each of the red #4 and #10 fabrics, cut:
- 8 A squares

From each of the red #5, #6, #9, and #11 fabrics, cut:
- 4 D triangles
- 4 D reverse triangles

From the red #7 fabric, cut:
- 8 E triangles

From the red #8 fabric, cut:
- 4 A squares

From the blue #1 fabric (¼ yard), cut:
- 12 D triangles
- 12 D reverse triangles

From the blue #2 fabric, cut:
- 4 A squares

From the blue #3 fabric, cut:
- 32 C triangles

From the blue #4 fabric, cut:
- 8 B pieces

From the blue #5 fabric, cut:
- 4 B pieces

From the blue #6 fabric, cut:
- 8 A squares

From the blue #7 fabric, cut:
- 4 E triangles

From the blue #8 fabric, cut:
- 8 E triangles

From the navy solid fabric, cut:
- Four 2 × 42-inch binding strips

Piecing the Blocks

The step-by-step instructions that follow direct you in piecing one block, referring to the pieces simply by their letter names, such as A square, B piece, D reverse triangle, etc., as shown in **Diagram 1**. As you piece each block, you will also need to refer to the other blocks in **Diagram 1** and the **Fabric Key** for the three starburst block color variations. These diagrams label each piece with a color reference such as Y1 for yellow #1 fabric, B3 for blue #3 fabric, and R7 for red #7 fabric. You will be making four corner blocks, four side blocks, and one center block.

1. To make one block, first lay out all pieces to make sure you have the correct color combination. Then sew C triangles to the slanted sides of the B pieces as shown in **Diagram 2**. Press the seam allowances toward the B pieces.

Diagram 2

2. Sew the B/C units and A squares together in three horizontal rows as shown in **Diagram 3**. Press the seam allowances toward the A squares. Join the three rows. Press the seam allowances to one side.

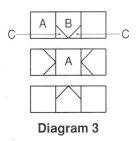

Diagram 3

3. Referring to **Diagram 4,** sew a D and a D reverse piece to the long sides of each E piece. Press seam allowances toward D pieces. Sew a triangular D/E unit to two opposite sides of the center unit from Step 2. Press seams away from the center unit. Join the remaining two triangular units to the center unit and press.

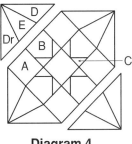

Diagram 4

4. Repeat to make a total of nine starburst blocks, paying careful attention to color placement within each block.

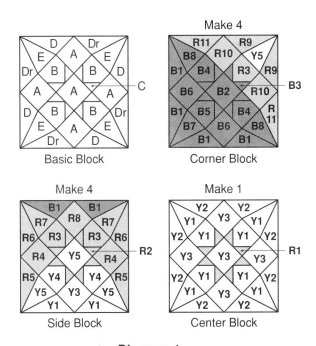

Diagram 1

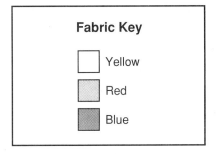

Assembling the Quilt Top

1. Sew the blocks together in three rows with three blocks in each row, referring to the **Quilt Diagram** for color placement of the blocks. Press the seam allowances in opposite directions from row to row.

2. Join the rows. Press the seam allowances to one side.

Quilting and Finishing

1. Mark quilting designs as desired. The quilt pictured was quilted in straight lines radiating from the center.

2. Layer the quilt back, batting, and quilt top; baste. Trim the quilt back and batting so they are approximately 3 inches larger than the quilt top on all sides.

3. Quilt all marked designs.

4. From the navy solid fabric, make approximately 150 inches of French-fold binding. See page 164 for suggested binding widths and instructions on making and attaching binding.

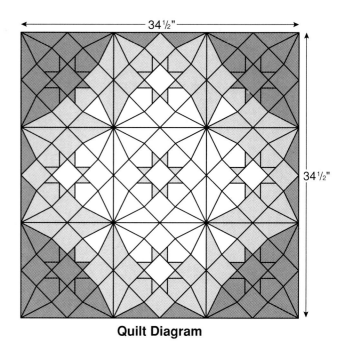

Quilt Diagram

5. Sew the binding to the quilt. Trim the excess batting and backing, and hand finish the binding on the wrong side of the quilt. Refer to page 167 for adding a hanging sleeve.

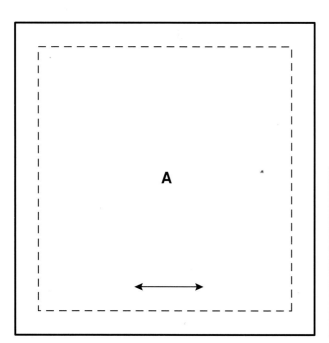

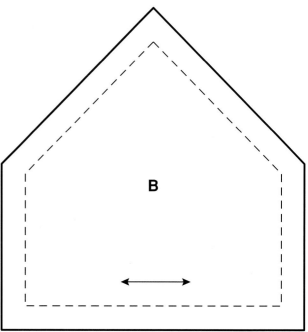

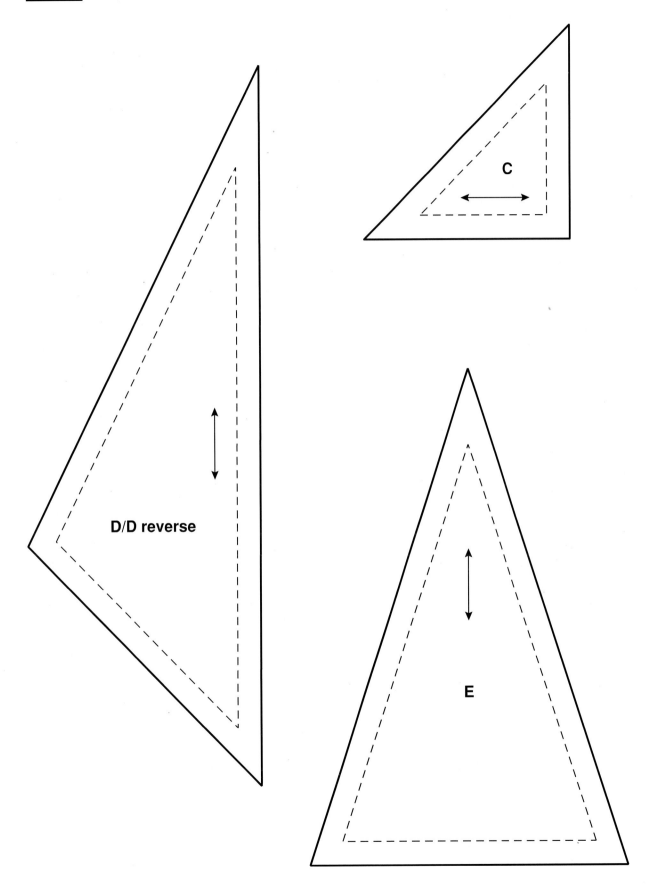

C

D/D reverse

E

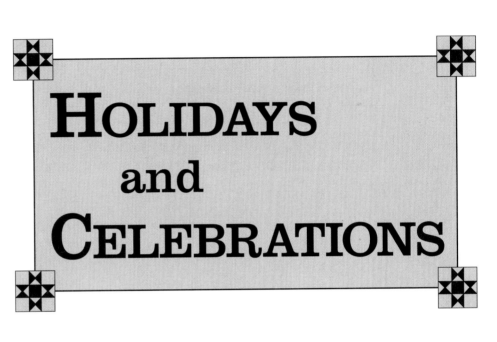

HOLIDAYS and CELEBRATIONS

Blazing Star Table Runner

Quiltmaker: Cyndi Hershey

Set the stage for festive entertaining with this table runner featuring glittering green lamé and gold metallic thread. Cyndi's elegant Blazing Star design has an unexpected twist—the points of the enlarged center block extend beyond the runner's straight edges. While this sparkling centerpiece is sure to draw compliments from your guests, you don't have to use it just for show. The lamé not only looks good but it's also washable.

Skill Level: Easy

Size: Finished runner is approximately
20 × 56½ inches
Finished blocks are 12 and 16 inches square

Fabrics and Supplies

✓ 1 yard of Christmas print fabric for setting triangles and patchwork

✓ ⅝ yard of red print fabric for patchwork and binding

✓ ¼ yard of green lamé fabric for patchwork

✓ ¼ yard of off-white solid fabric for patchwork

✓ 1¾ yards of fabric for quilt back

✓ ½ yard of 22-inch-wide *woven* fusible interfacing for lamé

✓ Crib-size quilt batting (45 × 60 inches)

✓ Rotary cutter, ruler, and mat

✓ Template plastic

✓ Gold metallic thread for quilting (optional)

Cutting

All measurements include a ¼-inch seam allowance. The instructions are written for quick-cutting the setting triangles with a rotary cutter and ruler. Prepare plastic templates for A and B pieces using patterns on pages 115–116. You will need to make A and B templates for both sizes of the block. Instructions for making and using templates are on page 153. Mark the pieces with the right side of the template facing you. Turn the templates over so the wrong side is facing you to mark the reverse pieces.

Following the manufacturer's instructions, fuse the interfacing to the wrong side of the lamé before cutting out the pieces to prevent fraying. You may want to cut just enough pieces to make one block to test your templates, cutting, and seam allowances for accuracy before cutting all your fabric.

From the Christmas print fabric, cut:
• 4 setting triangles

Cut one 18¼-inch square. Cut the square in half diagonally in both directions to make four triangles.

• 4 large A reverse pieces
• 4 large B reverse pieces
• 8 small A reverse pieces
• 8 small B reverse pieces

From the red print fabric, cut:
• 4 large B pieces
• 8 small A pieces
• Reserve the remaining fabric for binding

From the green lamé fabric, cut:
• 4 large A pieces
• 8 small B pieces

From the off-white solid fabric, cut:
• 4 large B and 4 large B reverse pieces
• 8 small B and 8 small B reverse pieces

Piecing the Blocks

The block is made by piecing the A and B pieces to form four large triangles and then joining the triangles together.

1. Referring to the **Fabric Key** on page 114 and the **Center Star Block Diagram**, lay out the large A and B pieces for the large Blazing Star block.

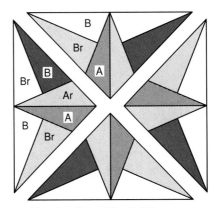

Center Star Block Diagram

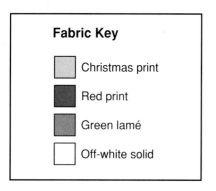

Fabric Key

- Christmas print
- Red print
- Green lamé
- Off-white solid

2. Join four green lamé A pieces and four Christmas print A reverse pieces along their long edges to make four A units, as shown in **Diagram 1A.** Press seams away from lamé.

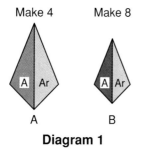

Make 4   Make 8

A   Ar   A   Ar

A   B

Diagram 1

3. Join four Christmas print B reverse pieces and four off-white print B pieces to make four B units, as shown in **Diagram 2A.** Press seam allowances toward the Christmas print. Sew these units to the lamé side of the A units.

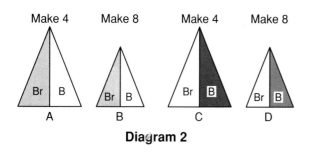

Make 4   Make 8   Make 4   Make 8

Br   B   Br   B   Br   B   Br   B

A   B   C   D

Diagram 2

4. Join four off-white print B reverse pieces and four red print B pieces to make four B units, as shown in **Diagram 2C.** Sew these B units to the Christmas print side of the A units to complete four large triangles.

5. Join the pieced triangles in pairs to make larger triangles. Join the larger triangles to complete the block.

6. Make two small Blazing Star blocks in the same manner, using the small A and B pieces. Refer to **Diagrams 1B, 2B, 2D,** and the **Assembly Diagram** for color combinations for the small end blocks.

Assembling the Runner

1. Referring to the **Assembly Diagram,** sew a setting triangle to one side of each of the small blocks to make Rows 1 and 3. Press seam allowances toward the setting triangles.

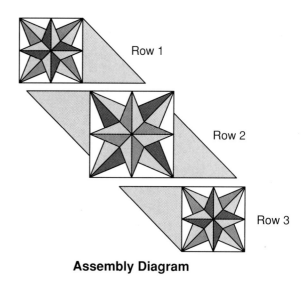

Row 1

Row 2

Row 3

Assembly Diagram

2. Sew setting triangles to two opposite sides of the large block, aligning the corner of one to the top left corner of the block, and the corner of the other to the bottom right corner of the block, to make Row 2. Note that the block is longer than the triangles. This will allow the Blazing Star points to extend beyond the edges of the finished table runner. Press seam allowances toward the setting triangles.

3. Join the rows, matching the block/triangle seam intersections. Here again, the setting triangles will not extend all the way to the end of the center block.

Quilting and Finishing

1. Layer the backing, batting, and table runner top; baste. Trim the backing and batting so they are approximately 3 inches larger than the table runner on all sides.

2. Quilt as desired. The table runner shown was machine quilted with gold metallic thread. The sections of the stars were quilted in the ditch, and the setting triangles were quilted with lines radiating from the star points.

3. From the red print fabric, make approximately 140 inches of French-fold binding. See page 164 for suggested binding widths and instructions on making and attaching binding.

4. Sew the binding to the table runner top. Trim excess batting and backing, and hand finish the binding on the wrong side of the runner.

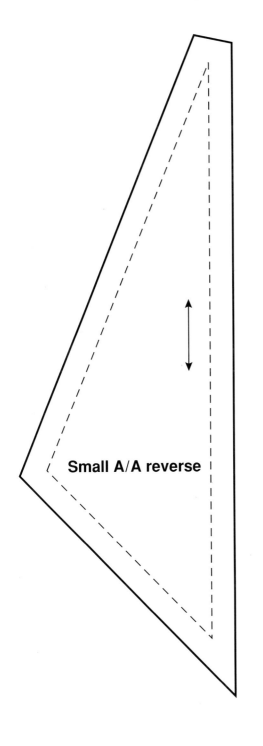

Small A/A reverse

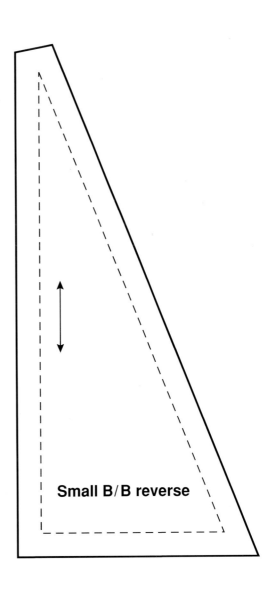

Small B/B reverse

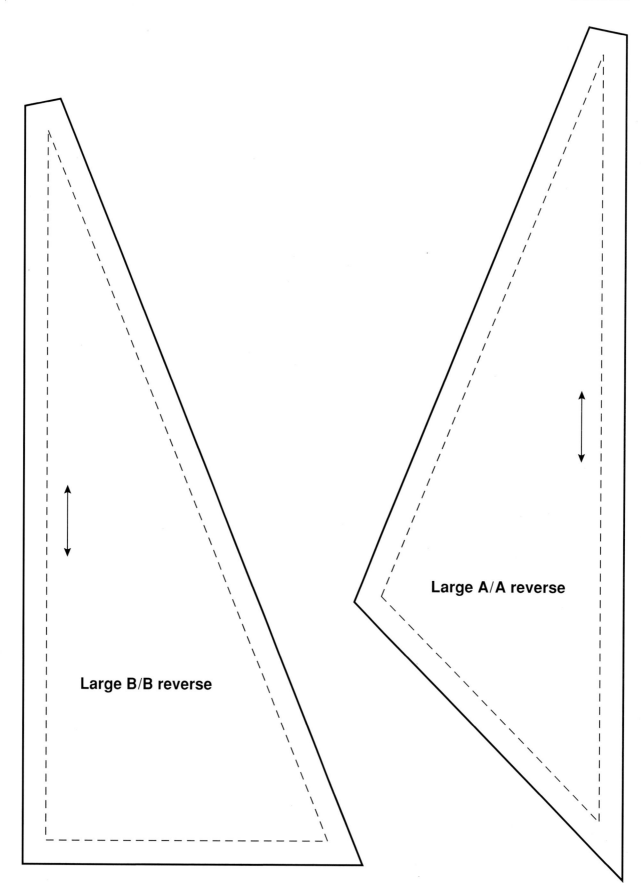

Large B/B reverse

Large A/A reverse

Watermelon Wedges

Designer: Mary Jane Cogan; Maker: Janet Coffman

What summertime picnic would be complete without the refreshing taste of watermelon? Whether it's Memorial Day, Labor Day, or the Fourth of July, this cheerful watermelon tablecloth and coordinating toss pillows will liven up your celebrations. All are easy to piece from squares and triangles sewn together into rows. Washable synthetic suede adds dimension and a touch of whimsy when cut into seed shapes and machine appliquéd to the juicy slices. What a treat!

Skill Level: Easy

Size: Finished tablecloth is 48 inches
square
Finished pillows are approximately 10 inches
long

Fabrics and Supplies for the Tablecloth and Two Pillows

✓ 1½ yards of white solid fabric for background patchwork

✓ 1 yard of dark green print fabric for border, patchwork, and binding

✓ ¾ yard of red print fabric for patchwork

✓ ⅔ yard of light green print fabric for patchwork

✓ Scrap of black synthetic suede (or other black solid fabric) for watermelon seeds

✓ Scrap of paper-backed fusible webbing

✓ 3 yards of fabric for quilt back

✓ Twin-size quilt batting (72 × 90 inches)

✓ Polyester fiberfill

✓ Rotary cutter, ruler, and mat

Cutting

All measurements include ¼-inch seam allowances. Measurements for the borders are longer than needed; trim them to the exact length before adding them to the quilt top. The instructions are written for quick-cutting the pieces using a rotary cutter and ruler. Cut all strips across the fabric width. Note that for some of the pieces, the quick-cutting method will result in leftover strips of fabric.

If you wish to use traditional cutting methods, make a 2½-inch template for the square. For the triangle, make a 2⅞-inch square. Cut the square in half diagonally to make a triangle to trace for your template. You may want to cut just enough pieces to make one watermelon section or pillow to test your templates, cutting, and seam allowances for accuracy. If your small watermelon does not measure approximately 10 inches, you can make adjustments before cutting all of your fabric.

From the white solid fabric, cut:
• 268 squares
Cut seventeen 2½-inch strips. Cut the strips into 2½-inch squares.

• 56 triangles
Cut two 2⅞-inch strips. Cut 28 squares, each 2⅞ inches square. Cut each square in half diagonally to make two triangles.

From the dark green print fabric, cut:
• Five 2½-inch border strips

• 16 squares
Cut one 2½-inch strip. Cut the strip into 2½-inch squares.

• 56 triangles
Cut two 2⅞-inch strips. Cut 28 squares, each 2⅞ inches square. Cut each square in half diagonally to make two triangles.

• Reserve the remaining fabric for binding

From the red print fabric, cut:
• 96 squares
Cut six 2½-inch strips. Cut the strips into 2½-inch squares.

• 48 triangles
Cut two 2⅞-inch strips. Cut 24 squares, each 2⅞ inches square. Cut each square in half diagonally to make two triangles.

From the light green print fabric, cut:
• 60 squares
Cut four 2½-inch strips. Cut the strips into 2½-inch squares.

• 64 triangles
Cut three 2⅞-inch strips. Cut 32 squares, each 2⅞ inches square. Cut each square in half diagonally to make two triangles.

Making the Triangle-Squares

Referring to the **Fabric Key** and the chart for the number of triangle-squares to piece of each color combination, sew pairs of triangles together. See **Diagram 1.** Press the seam allowances toward the darker fabric.

Triangle-Square
Diagram 1

TRIANGLE-SQUARES COLOR COMBINATIONS

Colors	Tablecloth	Pillows
Red/white	24	—
Light green/white	16	—
Light green/red	16	8
Light green/dark green	12	12
Dark green/white	16	—

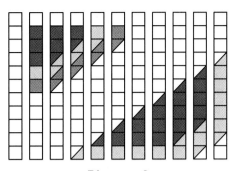

Diagram 3

Fabric Key

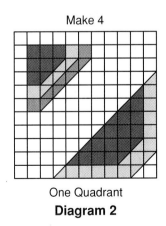

☐ White solid

▨ Dark green print

▨ Red print

▨ Light green print

3. Join the rows. Press the seam allowances to one side.

4. Make four quadrants. Join the quadrants referring to the **Quilt Diagram.** The heavy lines on the diagram define the quadrants.

Making the Tablecloth

Piecing and Assembling the Top

1. Lay out the squares and triangle-squares for one quadrant of the tablecloth top, as shown in **Diagram 2.**

Make 4

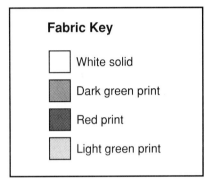

One Quadrant

Diagram 2

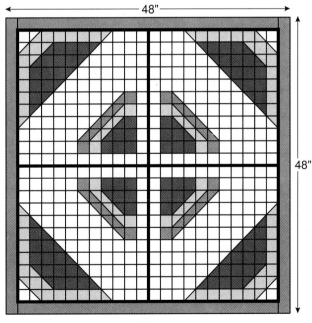

48"

48"

Quilt Diagram

2. Referring to **Diagram 3,** sew the pieces together in rows. Press the seam allowances in alternate directions from row to row.

5. Using the seed pattern on page 121, trace 32 watermelon seeds onto the paper side of the fusible webbing. Following the manufacturer's instructions, fuse the webbing onto the wrong side of the black synthetic suede or fabric. Cut out the seeds. Fuse three seeds on the red section of each small watermelon and five seeds on the red section of each large watermelon. Machine satin stitch around the seeds.

6. Cut one dark green border strip into four 10-inch lengths. Sew a 10-inch piece to the end of each of the four remaining border strips. Follow the directions with **Diagram 33** on page 165 for joining your border strips.

7. Measure the width of the tablecloth top. Trim two borders to this length (approximately 44½ inches). Sew borders to the top and bottom edges of the tablecloth. Press the seam allowances toward the borders.

8. Measure the length of the tablecloth top, including the top and bottom borders. Trim two borders to this length (approximately 48½ inches). Sew borders to the sides of the tablecloth. Press the seam allowances toward the borders.

Quilting and Finishing

1. Mark quilting designs onto the quilt top. Refer to the photo on page 117 for the placement of diagonal lines of quilting.

2. Cut the backing fabric into two 1½-yard pieces. Cut one piece in half lengthwise. Sew a half panel to each long side of the full panel. Press the seam allowances toward the outer panels.

3. Layer the backing, batting, and tablecloth; baste. Trim the quilt back and batting so they are approximately 3 inches larger than the quilt top on all sides.

4. Quilt all marked designs. The quilt pictured is machine quilted in the ditch around each colored area of the watermelon slices. Meander quilting gives texture to the red areas. See "Machine Quilting Tips" on this page for how-to details.

MACHINE QUILTING TIPS

If you plan to machine quilt your project, here are a few quick tips for better results.

1. Pin baste your layers together with safety pins rather than hand basting with thread. Machine quilting stitches are close together and make removing basting thread more difficult. Simply remove the safety pins before stitching in that area.

2. To meander quilt, you need to be able to move the quilt layers freely in a random pattern. To do this, lower your machine's feed dogs and use a darning foot rather than your regular presser foot.

3. To begin stitching, lower your needle through all layers of your quilt. Raise the needle and pull on the top thread until a loop of bobbin thread comes through the quilt. Pull the bobbin thread completely to the top side of your quilt so it won't get tangled and stitched over on the back side.

4. Plan ahead. With meander quilting, your stitching pattern will look like oversized jigsaw puzzle pieces. The design is not marked on the quilt; it is simply stitched "by eye." To keep lines of stitching from crossing over one another, you will need to plan where to begin and where to end so you don't stitch yourself into a corner. ◆

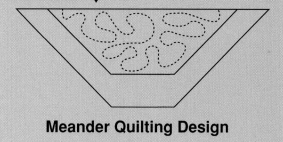

Meander Quilting Design

5. Make approximately 200 inches of French-fold binding from the dark green fabric. See page 164 for instructions on making and attaching binding.

6. Sew the binding to the quilt top. Trim the excess batting and backing, and hand finish the binding to the wrong side of the tablecloth. Optional: If you prefer to use Watermelon Wedges as a wallhanging rather than a table-cloth, see page 167 for directions on attaching a hanging sleeve.

Making the Pillows

1. Referring to **Diagram 4,** lay out the squares and triangle-squares in rows to make one pillow front.

2. Join the pieces in rows. Press the seam allowances in alternate directions from row to row. Join the rows. **Diagram 5** shows the pillow front assembled. Press the seam allowances to one side.

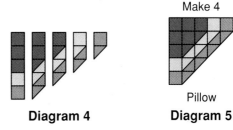

Make 4

Pillow

Diagram 4　　**Diagram 5**

3. Prepare and machine appliqué three watermelon seeds to the red section of the pillow front. Instructions for making and adding seeds are in Step 5 of "Making the Tablecloth."

4. Repeat Steps 1 through 3 to make three more pillow sections.

5. Stitch two pillow sections together with right sides facing and raw edges aligned, leaving an opening for turning.

6. Turn the pillow. Stuff with fiberfill. Stitch the opening closed.

7. Repeat Steps 5 and 6 to make a second pillow.

**Watermelon
Seed Pattern**

Christmas in July

Quiltmaker: Margie N. Bergan

Named for Margie's family's annual holiday get-together, this quilt is so spectacular it will make you want to celebrate Christmas every month of the year. Its Log Cabin-style trees and three variations of stars are set on point atop a field of bright Christmas roses. Trimmed in a pieced border of vivid red and green, this festive quilt is a real holiday showstopper.

Skill Level: Challenging

Size: Finished quilt is 93½ inches square Finished Star and Tree block is 18 inches square (approximately 25½ inches on the diagonal)

Fabrics and Supplies

✓ 6¼ yards of red-and-green floral print fabric for setting pieces, sashing, border patchwork, and patchwork blocks

✓ 2½ yards of bright red print fabric for border patchwork, sashing strips, and binding

✓ 2 yards of dark green print fabric for border patchwork and patchwork tree blocks

✓ 1¼ yards of cream solid fabric for patchwork blocks

✓ ½ yard of medium beige print fabric for patchwork blocks

✓ ¼ yard of gold-star print fabric for small sashing squares (Stars are approximately 1 inch across; squares for stars are cut 1½ inches. Extra fabric is allowed for centering the stars in the squares.)

✓ ⅛ yard, or scraps, of brown print fabric for tree trunks

✓ 8½ yards of fabric for quilt back

✓ King-size quilt batting (120 inches square)

✓ Rotary cutter, ruler, and mat

✓ Template plastic (optional)

Cutting

All measurements include a ¼-inch seam allowance. Instructions given are for quick-cutting the pieces with a rotary cutter and ruler. Cut all strips across the fabric width unless directed otherwise. A quick-piecing method for making the patchwork for the small and large stars is used. A strip method is used for making the tree portion of the Log Cabin Tree blocks.

You may want to cut just enough pieces to make one block to test your cutting and seam allowances for accuracy. If your finished block does not measure the size stated above, you can make adjustments before cutting all your fabric.

Tip: *This quilt requires cutting many different pieces. For best results, label pieces as you cut them to make identification easier later on.* ★

From the red-and-green floral print fabric, cut:
● One 95-inch lengthwise piece for setting triangles

  #### From this piece, cut:
  ● Two 22⅛-inch squares. Cut each square in half diagonally to make four corner setting triangles.
  ● One 35¼-inch square. Cut the square in half diagonally both ways to make four side setting triangles.

From the remaining red-and-green floral print fabric, cut:
● Ten 4½-inch strips for sashing

  #### From these strips, cut:
  ● Four 4½ × 18½-inch sashing strips
  ● Four 4½ × 28½-inch sashing strips
  ● Eight 4½ × 19½-inch sashing strips

● Fourteen 3½-inch strips for border strip sets

● 72 A triangles
  Cut two 3¼-inch strips. Cut the strips into 18 squares, each 3¼ inches square. If you're using the quick-piecing method for the triangle units for small patchwork stars, leave the squares as is. If you're using traditional piecing, cut each square in half diagonally in both directions to make four triangles.

● 9 B squares
  Cut one 2½-inch strip. Cut the strip into nine 2½-inch squares.

● 40 G triangles
  Cut two 7¼-inch strips. From the strips, cut ten 7¼-inch squares. If you're using the quick-piecing method for the triangle units for large patchwork stars, leave the squares as is. If you're using traditional piecing, cut each square in half diagonally in both directions to make four triangles.

● 4 corner triangles
  Cut two 5⅛-inch squares. Cut the squares diagonally to make two triangles.

From the bright red print fabric, cut:
- Seven 3½-inch strips for border strip sets
- Twenty-two 1½-inch strips for sashing
    ### From these strips, cut:
    - Twenty 1½ × 18½-inch sashing strips
    - Eight 1½ × 23½-inch sashing strips
    - Four 1½ × 28½-inch sashing strips
- Reserve the remaining fabric for binding

From the dark green print fabric, cut:
- Fourteen 3½-inch strips for border strip sets
- 60 D rectangles and 60 F rectangles
    Cut ten 1½-inch strips. From these strips, cut 60 D rectangles, 1½ × 2½ inches, and 60 F rectangles, 1½ × 3½ inches.

From the cream solid fabric, cut:
- 72 A triangles
    Cut two 3¼-inch strips. Cut the strips into eighteen 3¼-inch squares. If you're using the quick-piecing method for the triangle units for small patchwork stars, leave the squares as is. If you're using traditional piecing, cut each square in half diagonally in both directions to make four triangles.
- 20 B squares
    Cut two 2½-inch strips. Cut the strips into twenty 2½-inch squares.
- 20 G triangles
    Cut one 7¼-inch strip. Cut the strip into five 7¼-inch squares. If you're using the quick-piecing method for the triangle units for large patchwork stars, leave the squares as is. If you're using traditional piecing, cut each square in half diagonally in both directions to make four triangles.
- 20 E triangles
    Cut one 3⅞-inch strip. Cut the strip into ten 3⅞-inch squares. Cut each square in half diagonally to make two triangles.
- 56 C squares
    Cut two 1½-inch strips. Cut the strips into 1½-inch squares.
- 56 D rectangles
    Cut four 1½-inch strips. Cut the strips into 1½ × 2½-inch rectangles.
- 40 F rectangles
    Cut four 1½-inch strips. Cut the strips into 1½ × 3½-inch rectangles.

From the medium beige print fabric, cut:
- 20 G triangles

Cut one 7¼-inch strip. Cut the strip into five 7¼-inch squares. If you're using the quick-piecing method for the triangle units for large patchwork stars, leave the squares as is. If you're using traditional piecing, cut each square in half diagonally in both directions to make four triangles.
- 20 E triangles
    Cut one 3⅞-inch strip. Cut the strip into ten 3⅞-inch squares. Cut each square in half diagonally to make two triangles.

From the gold-star print fabric, cut:
- 32 C squares
    Cut two 1½-inch strips. Cut the strips into 1½-inch squares.

From the brown print fabric, cut:
- Two 1½-inch strips. Cut the strips into 20 rectangles, each 1½ × 3 inches, for tree trunks.

Fabric Key

▦	Red-and-green floral print	⣿	Medium beige print
■	Red print	▨	Gold-star print
▨	Dark green print	‖	Brown print
☐	Cream solid		

Making the Small Star Blocks

There are two types of small star blocks in the quilt shown, five like **Diagram 1** and four like **Diagram 2**. Both types of star blocks are made with four-triangle units, as indicated by the heavy lines.

Make 5

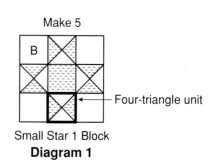

Small Star 1 Block
Diagram 1

Four-triangle unit

Make 4

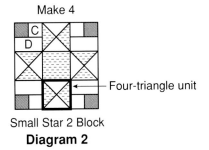

Four-triangle unit

Small Star 2 Block
Diagram 2

Quick-Piecing Four-Triangle Units

If you are using traditional piecing methods, refer to the **Fabric Key** and join A triangles as shown in **Diagram 3** to make 36 four-triangle units. For quick-piecing, follow the steps below to assemble the four-triangle units for all nine of the small star blocks.

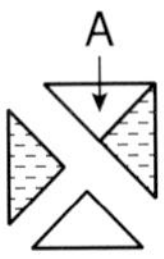

A

Traditional Piecing
Diagram 3

1. Place two 3¼-inch squares (one floral print and one cream solid) right sides together.

2. Using a pencil, draw a diagonal line from corner to corner in both directions. Stitch ¼ inch from each side of one diagonal line only (see **Diagram 4**). Cut on the drawn line between the stitching to make two triangle-square units. Press the seam allowances toward the darker fabric.

Diagram 4

3. Extend the drawn line on the wrong side of one of the triangle-squares as shown in **Diagram 5** so the line reaches from corner to corner.

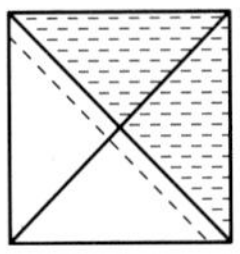

Diagram 5

4. Place the two triangle-squares right sides together *with contrasting triangles facing,* raw edges aligned, and marked unit on top. Stitch ¼ inch from each side of the marked line as shown in **Diagram 6.** Cut on the diagonal line between rows of stitching. You will have 2 four-triangle units. Press the seam allowances in one direction. Repeat Steps 1 through 4 to make a total of 36 four-triangle units.

Stitch   Cut   Press open

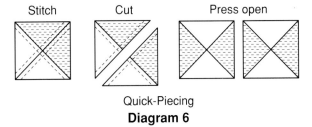

Quick-Piecing
Diagram 6

Piecing the Small Star 1 Blocks

1. Lay out 4 four-triangle units, one floral print B square, and four cream B squares in three rows, as shown in **Diagram 7.**

2. Join the pieces to make horizontal rows. Press the seam allowances toward the B squares. Join the rows to complete a Small Star 1 block. Repeat to make a total of five blocks.

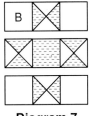

Diagram 7

Piecing the Small Star 2 Blocks

1. Join one cream C square and one gold-star C square. Press the seam allowances toward the darker fabric. Repeat to make 16 units.

2. Sew a cream D rectangle to one side of each cream/star unit to make a square. Make eight squares as shown in **Diagram 8A** and eight as shown in **Diagram 8B.**

Make 8   Make 8

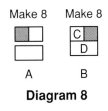

A   B
Diagram 8

3. Lay out 4 four-triangle units, one floral print B square, two **Diagram 8A** squares, and two **Diagram 8B** squares, arranging them in three horizontal rows, as shown in **Diagram 9.** Join the units to create the rows. Press the seam allowances away from the four-triangle units. Join the rows to make one Small Star 2 block. Repeat to make a total of four Small Star 2 blocks.

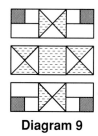

Diagram 9

Making the Log Cabin Tree Blocks

1. Prepare the 20 brown print rectangles for the tree trunks for appliqué by turning under ¼ inch along each long edge.

2. Position a trunk strip on a cream E triangle as shown in **Diagram 10.** Center and appliqué the strip to the cream triangle. Trim excess brown fabric even with the raw edges of the E triangle. Repeat to make a total of 20 trunk units. Sew each tree trunk triangle to a beige print E triangle. Press the seam allowances toward the beige print triangle. Repeat to make a total of 20 trunk units as shown in **Diagram 10.**

Trim brown edges even with edges of E triangle | Add medium beige triangle | Trunk unit

Diagram 10

3. Referring to **Diagram 11,** lay out one trunk unit, with dark green print and cream solid C, D, and F pieces to form one tree.

Make 20

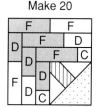

Log Cabin Tree Block
Diagram 11

4. Join half of the cream C, D, and F pieces to dark green D rectangles. Sew the other cream pieces to dark green F rectangles. Press the seams toward the dark green fabric. Referring to **Diagram 12,** sew a C/D unit to one side of the tree trunk unit; sew a C/F unit to the adjacent side. Continue in the same manner adding pieces to alternate sides. Press the seam allowances away from the trunk unit as you add pieces. Repeat to make a total of 20 Log Cabin Tree blocks.

Diagram 12

Making the Large Star Blocks

If you are using traditional piecing methods, join G triangles as shown in **Diagram 13** to make 20 four-triangle units. For quick-piecing, the same method used to quick-piece the small four-triangle units can be used to make larger four-triangle units for the large stars. Note that these stars use three fabrics rather than two, however.

1. Using five 7¼-inch cream and five floral print squares, follow **Diagrams 4** and **5** and the "Quick-Piecing Four-Triangle Units" directions on page 125 to make ten triangle-square units.

2. Following Step 1 above, use beige print squares and floral print squares to make ten beige/floral triangle-square units.

3. Place a cream/floral triangle-square unit right sides together with a beige/floral unit making sure the floral print is against the lighter fabric, as shown in **Diagram 6.** Use a ruler and pencil to extend the diagonal line from corner to corner. Stitch ¼ inch from each side of drawn line. Cut on the line to make two four-triangle units as shown in **Diagram 13.** Repeat to make a total of 20 units.

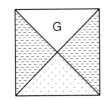

Large Four-Triangle Unit
Diagram 13

4. Referring to **Diagram 14,** lay out one Small Star 1 block, four Log Cabin Tree blocks, and four large four-triangle units in three horizontal rows as shown, paying close attention to the diagram for color placement.

Make 5

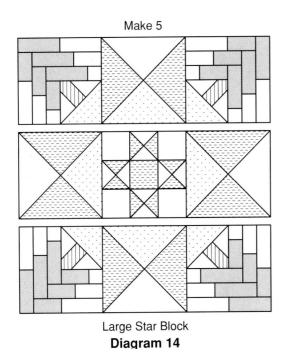

Large Star Block
Diagram 14

5. Join the blocks and units into rows. Press the seams toward the four-triangle units. Join the rows. Repeat to make a total of five Large Star blocks.

Assembling the Inner Quilt Top

Making the Quilt Center Section

1. Referring to **Diagram 15,** sew a red print 18½-inch sashing strip to each long side of the corresponding floral rectangle. Press the seam allowances toward the red strips. Repeat to make a total of four sashing strips.

Make 4

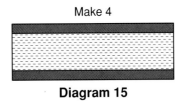

Diagram 15

2. Lay out one Large Star block, the four sashing strips, and the four Small Star 2 blocks, as shown in **Diagram 16.**

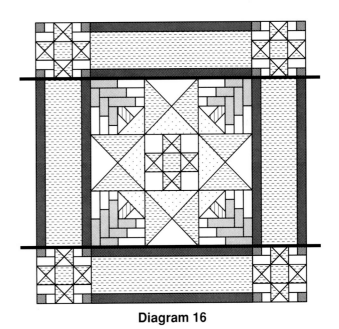

Diagram 16

3. Join the pieces into three horizontal rows to make the quilt center. The heavy lines on the diagram indicate the rows. Press the seam allowances toward the sashing pieces.

4. Join the rows. Press the seam allowances away from the center block.

Constructing the Corner Sections

1. Sew a 1½-inch gold-star C square to one end of eight of the 18½-inch red strips.

2. Sew these sashing strips to the 19½-inch floral print rectangles to make four strips as shown in **Diagram 17A** and four as shown in **Diagram 17B**. Press the seam allowances toward the red strips.

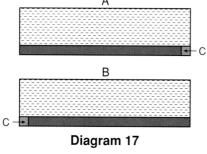

Diagram 17

Diagram 18

3. Referring to **Diagram 18**, sew an 18½-inch red sashing strip to one side of each of the four remaining Large Star blocks. Press the seam allowances toward the red strips.

4. Sew the sashing strips made in Step 2 to the opposite sides of each block as shown in **Diagram 18**. Press seams away from the blocks.

5. Sew a 28½-inch red strip to one side of a 28½-inch floral print strip. Press the seam allowances toward the red strip. Repeat to make a total of four of these strips. Sew one of these sashing strips to each of the four Large Star blocks, referring to **Diagram 19** for placement.

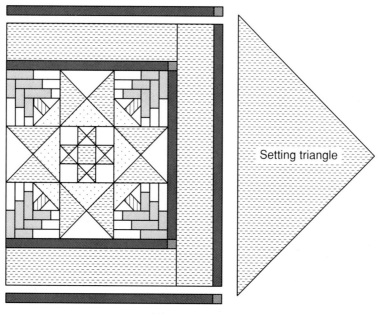

Setting triangle

Diagram 19

6. Sew a 1½-inch gold-star C square to one end of each of the eight 23½-inch red strips. Press the seams toward the squares. Referring to **Diagram 19,** sew these sashing strips to two opposite sides of each Large Star block. Press the seam allowances toward the red strips.

7. Sew a floral print corner setting triangle to the side of the block *opposite* the side that has no sashing strips (see **Diagram 19**). Press the seam allowances toward the corner triangle. Repeat for all four blocks.

8. Referring to **Diagram 20,** sew floral print side setting triangles to the two opposite sides of *two* of the corner units as shown.

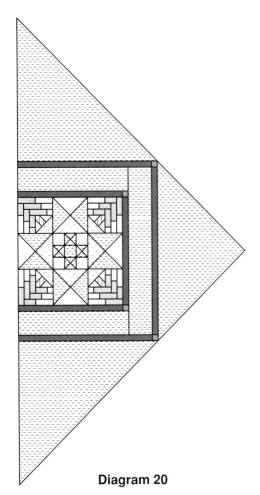

Diagram 20

Joining the Units

1. Referring to the **Quilt Diagram** on page 130, sew a corner unit (without side triangles) to two opposite sides of the quilt center. The heavy lines indicate the quilt sections. Press the seams away from the center unit.

2. Sew the two corner units with side triangles to the remaining two sides of the quilt top. Press the seams away from the center.

Adding the Borders

1. Using the 3½-inch floral print, green print, and red print fabric strips, make seven strip sets, referring to **Diagram 21** for color placement. Press the seam allowances away from the red strip.

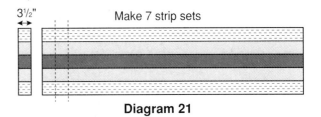

3½"   Make 7 strip sets

Diagram 21

2. Cut 3½-inch segments from the strip sets. Each set will produce 12 segments.

3. Join 17 segments, off-setting the segments as shown in **Diagram 22.** From an additional border segment, remove a floral print square. Sew this shorter segment to the border strip as shown in the diagram to make one border strip. Repeat to make four border strips.

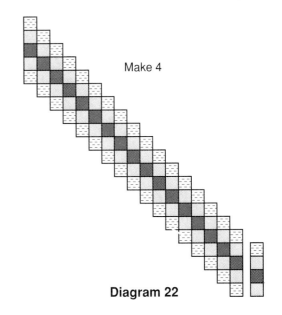

Make 4

Diagram 22

Quilt Diagram

4. To make partial segments for the border corners, remove a floral square from four border segments and discard. Remove a green and a floral square from four border segments to make three-square and two-square segments. Lay out these partial segments as shown in **Diagram 23,** and sew them together to form a corner unit. Sew the corner unit to one end of each border, as shown in **Diagram 24.**

Make 4

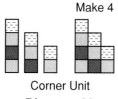

Corner Unit
Diagram 23

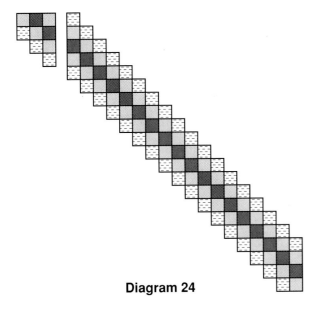

Diagram 24

5. Using a rotary cutter and ruler, trim the two long uneven edges of the pieced borders, making sure you leave a ¼-inch seam allowance extending beyond the corners of the green squares. See **Diagram 25.**

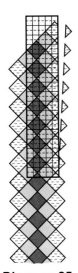

Diagram 25

6. Sew the outer borders to the quilt top. Your border strips will be longer than your quilt length. *Do not cut off excess fabric.* The extra length will be needed to miter the corners of the borders. Press the seam allowances toward the borders. Miter the border corner seams, referring to page 160 for more detailed directions.

7. Sew a floral print corner triangle to each outside corner of the quilt top.

Quilting and Finishing

1. Mark quilting designs as desired. The quilt pictured was outline quilted around the star blocks. The traditional tea cup motif was used in the large floral setting triangles, and the borders were quilted with double cross-hatching. This is achieved by quilting ¼ inch on each side of the pieced border seam lines. The effect is that of a plaid.

2. Cut the backing fabric into three equal lengths. Cut an 18-inch-wide panel from one of the lengths. Sew a wide panel to each side of the narrow panel. Press the seams away from the center panel.

3. Layer the quilt back, batting, and quilt top; baste. Trim the quilt back and batting so they are 3 inches larger than the quilt top on all sides.

4. Quilt all marked designs.

5. From the red print fabric, make approximately 395 inches of French-fold binding. See page 164 for suggested binding widths and instructions on making and attaching binding.

6. Sew the binding to the quilt top. Trim the excess batting and backing, and hand finish the binding on the wrong side of the quilt.

Christmas Rose

Quiltmaker: Mollie Fish

Achieve a vintage 1890s look by combining traditional red, green, and pink print fabrics appliquéd on muslin. The central appliqué block is the focal point for this quick but clever Christmas hanging that can really be displayed all year 'round. Freezer paper appliqué is a perfect technique for smooth curves, and strip sets make quick work of the checkerboard border.

Skill Level: Easy

Size: Finished quilt is 25½ inches square
Finished block is 13½ inches square

Fabrics and Supplies

✓ ⅔ yard of muslin or off-white fabric for border and background

✓ ⅝ yard of green print fabric for patchwork, appliqué, and binding

✓ ½ yard of red print fabric for patchwork and appliqué

✓ ¼ yard, or 7-inch-square scrap, of pink print fabric for appliqué

✓ 1 yard of fabric for quilt back

✓ Crib-size quilt batting (45 × 60 inches)

✓ Rotary cutter, ruler, and mat

✓ Plastic-coated freezer paper or template plastic

✓ Tracing paper

✓ Black permanent marker

✓ Index or recipe cards for circles (optional)

Cutting

All measurements include a ¼-inch seam allowance. The instructions are written for quick-cutting the background pieces and strips for strip sets with a rotary cutter and ruler. Cut all strips across the fabric width.

Patterns A, B, C, and D for appliqué flowers and leaves are on pages 135–136. The appliqué patterns are finished size; add seam allowances when you cut the pieces from fabric. Read through "Hand Appliqué" beginning on page 156 and choose the appliqué method you wish to prepare the appliqués. Either make plastic templates to mark and cut the appliqué pieces or use freezer paper templates.

From the muslin or off-white fabric, cut:
• Four 4 × 14-inch borders
    Cut one 14-inch strip. Cut the rectangles from the strip.

• One 14-inch background square

• Four 6½-inch corner squares
    Cut one 6½-inch strip. Cut the squares from the strip.

From the green print fabric, cut:
• Two 2-inch strips for strip sets
• 4 A leaves
• Reserve the remaining fabric for D flower centers and binding

From the red print fabric, cut:
• Two 2-inch strips for strip sets
• 5 C flowers

From the pink print fabric, cut:
• 1 B flower

Making the Appliqué Sections

1. Make a master pattern for the center block to use as a guide for positioning the appliqué pieces on the background. Fold the 14-inch square of tracing paper in half horizontally, vertically, and diagonally in both directions, and lightly crease. Referring to the **Appliqué Block Diagram** for placement, trace around templates or patterns to make a full-size drawing. Darken the pattern outlines with a permanent marker.

Appliqué Block Diagram

Fabric Key

☐ Muslin

▨ Green print

▤ Red print

▧ Pink print

2. Position the master appliqué pattern under the 14-inch fabric square; pin the fabric square to the paper pattern.

3. Use the master pattern to help position the prepared A leaf appliqués on the background square; pin the appliqués in place, pinning only through the fabrics. Unpin the background square from the master pattern. Appliqué the four leaves in place.

4. In the same manner, position, pin, and appliqué the prepared pink B flower. Make sure,

CRISP APPLIQUÉ CIRCLES

For each circle you will be appliquéing, trace your finished size circle onto paper approximately the same weight as an index card. Use your D pattern piece to trace your circles, then cut them out. You can also use a spool, coin, or draftsman's circle template to trace circles. Use these index-card templates to mark and cut out your fabric circles. Mark circles on the wrong side of the fabric and add a scant ¼-inch seam allowance when cutting.

Run a basting thread around each fabric circle, sewing in the area between the drawn line and the raw edge. Position the paper template on the wrong side of the fabric circle. Pull on the basting thread to gather the fabric over the paper template. Tighten, and then make a few stitches to secure the gathers. Appliqué the circle in place. Turn the block to the wrong side and make a cut in the base fabric. Remove and discard the paper template. ♦

as you position the appliqué, that the B piece will overlap the raw edges at the base of the leaves. After appliquéing, turn the block to the wrong side; trim away the background fabric from behind the pink flower, trimming ¼ inch to the *inside* of the appliqué stitches.

5. In the same manner, position and appliqué the prepared red C flower atop the pink one. Trim from behind the red flower. Wait to add the green D flower center.

6. To make a corner flower square, fold and lightly crease a 6½-inch muslin square vertically and horizontally. Use the crease lines to center a red C flower on the square. Appliqué the C flower in place. Turn to the wrong side and trim from behind the appliqué. Repeat to make a total of four corner squares.

7. Refer to "Crisp Appliqué Circles" on this page and add green D flower centers to the large block and four corner squares. The finished diameter of the circle is 1½ inches.

Making the Checkerboard Border

1. Referring to the **Fabric Key** and **Strip Set Diagram,** use the red and green strips to make two strip sets. Press the seam allowances in one direction. Cut the strip sets into a total of 36 segments, each 2 inches wide.

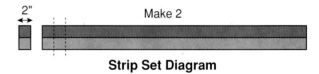

2" Make 2

Strip Set Diagram

2. Join nine segments to make a pieced checkerboard border strip, as shown in the **Quilt Assembly Diagram.** Repeat to make a total of four of these pieced strips.

Assembling the Quilt Top

1. To complete the border, sew a 4 × 14-inch muslin rectangle to each of the four checkerboard borders. Press the seam allowances toward the muslin.

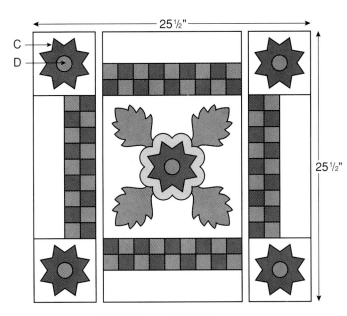

Quilt Assembly Diagram

2. Sew a border to the top and bottom of the center block. Press the seams toward the center block. Sew the appliqué corner squares to the ends of the two remaining borders. Press

the seam allowances toward the corner squares. Sew the borders to the quilt.

Quilting and Finishing

1. Mark quilting designs. The quilt shown was machine quilted with outline stitching around the appliqués and along the patchwork seams. Diagonal line quilting was used in the quilt center and corner blocks background muslin areas. Straight line quilting was used in the top, bottom, and side borders.

2. Layer the quilt back, batting, and quilt top; baste. Trim the quilt back and batting so they are approximately 3 inches larger than the quilt top on all sides. Quilt as marked.

3. From the green print fabric, make approximately 115 inches of French-fold binding. See page 164 for suggested binding widths and instructions on making and attaching binding.

4. Sew the binding to the quilt top. Trim excess batting and backing, and hand finish the binding on the back of the quilt. See page 167 for instructions for making a hanging sleeve.

A

Pattern is finished size.
Add seam allowance when
cutting pieces from fabric.

B

C

Patterns are finished size.
Add seam allowances when
cutting pieces from fabric.

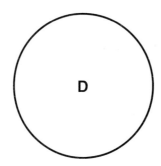

D

Sapphire's Window

Quiltmaker: Mary Jane Cogan

A variety of miniature prints in rich fall colors creates this fabric picture, perfect for autumn or Halloween decorating. This small wallhanging is made primarily of 1¼-inch squares, making it a pictorial quilt easy enough for a beginner to piece. Mary Jane made her cat black and named the project for Sapphire, her beloved pet of 17 years. You can work up the quilt in the colors shown here or choose fabric the color of your favorite cat.

Skill Level: Easy

Size: Finished quilt is 20 × 27½ inches

Fabrics and Supplies

- ✓ ⅓ yard of dark gold print fabric for border and tree
- ✓ ¼ yard of orange print fabric for tree and pumpkin
- ✓ ¼ yard of black print fabric for cat
- ✓ ¼ yard of tan print fabric for ground
- ✓ ¼ yard, or scraps, of light gold print fabric for tree and windowsill
- ✓ ⅛ yard, or scraps, of brown print fabric for tree trunks and pumpkin stem
- ✓ ¼ yard, or scraps, of white print fabric for sky
- ✓ ⅔ yard of fabric for quilt back
- ✓ Quilt batting, larger than 20 × 27½ inches
- ✓ Rotary cutter, ruler, and mat

Cutting

All measurements include a ¼-inch seam allowance. The instructions are written for quick-cutting the squares and triangles with a rotary cutter and ruler. Cut all strips across the fabric.

From the dark gold print fabric, cut:
- Four 1¾-inch strips. Cut the strips into 88 squares, each 1¾ inches square.
  Note: If you prefer to use single strips of fabric for your quilt borders rather than piecing them from squares, you will only need to cut 16 squares. For single strip borders, cut three 1¾-inch strips.
- One 2⅛ × 5-inch strip. Cut two 2⅛-inch squares from the strip. Cut each square in half

diagonally to make two triangles. You will have one extra triangle.

From the orange print fabric, cut:
- Three 1¾-inch strips. Cut the strips into 61 squares, each 1¾ inches square.
- One 2⅛ × 9-inch strip. Cut four 2⅛-inch squares from the strip. Cut each square in half diagonally to make two triangles. You will have one extra triangle.

From the black print fabric, cut:
- Two 1¾-inch strips. Cut the strips into 34 squares, each 1¾ inches square.
- One 2⅛ × 9-inch strip. Cut four 2⅛-inch squares from the strip. Cut each square in half diagonally to make two triangles. You will have one extra triangle.

From the tan print fabric, cut:
- Two 1¾-inch strips. Cut the strips into 48 squares, each 1¾ inches square.
- One 2⅛ × 18-inch strip. Cut eight 2⅛-inch squares from the strip. Cut each square in half diagonally to make two triangles.

From the light gold print fabric, cut:
- Two 1¾-inch strips. Cut the strips into 42 squares, each 1¾ inches square.
- One 2⅛-inch square. Cut the square in half diagonally to make two triangles. You will have one extra triangle.

From the brown print fabric, cut:
- One 1¾-inch strip. Cut the strip into 11 squares, each 1¾ inches square.
- One 2⅛-inch square. Cut the square in half diagonally to make two triangles. You will have one extra triangle.

From the white print fabric, cut:
- Two 1¾-inch strips. Cut the strips into 49 squares, each 1¾ inches square.
- One 2⅛ × 5-inch strip. Cut two 2⅛-inch squares from the strip. Cut each square in half diagonally to make two triangles. You will have one extra triangle.

Piecing the Quilt

1. Referring to the **Fabric Key** and **Quilt Diagram,** lay out the squares and triangles for the quilt.

Fabric Key

- ▣ Dark gold print
- ░ Light gold print
- ▒ Orange print
- ▨ Brown print
- ■ Black print
- □ White print
- ▤ Tan print

2. Join the triangles to make triangle-squares, as shown. Press the seam allowances toward the darker fabrics.

Triangle-Square

3. Join the squares and triangle-squares in 22 horizontal rows. Note: If you are using single strips of fabric for your borders rather than piecing them with squares, you will only have 20 rows of squares. Press the seams in opposite directions from row to row. Join the rows.

4. If you've chosen to add the border as single strips of fabric, measure the width of your quilt through the center (approximately 18 inches) and cut one of the 1¾-inch dark gold strips into two pieces this length. Sew one strip to the top and one to the bottom of your quilt. For the side borders, measure the length of your quilt, including the top and bottom borders (approximately 28 inches) and trim the remaining two dark gold strips to this length. Sew one border strip to each side of the quilt. Press seam allowances toward the borders.

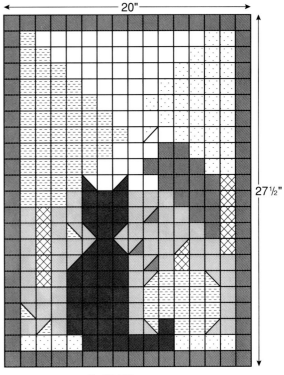

Quilt Diagram

Quilting and Finishing

1. Mark top for quilting, if desired. The quilt pictured was machine quilted in the ditch around the trees, cat, and pumpkin.

2. Lay out batting. Place the quilt back on top of the batting with the *wrong* side of fabric against the batting. Lay the quilt top with the *right* side facing the back so they're right sides together. Pin layers together along outside edge.

3. Stitch around outside edges using a ¼-inch seam, leaving an opening for turning.

4. Trim the back and batting even with the quilt top. Turn the quilt right side out. Hand stitch the opening closed.

5. Machine quilt as desired.

6. Refer to page 167 for making and adding a hanging sleeve.

Sawtooth Star Tree Skirt

Quiltmaker: Phyllis Dobbs

Sawtooth Star blocks set on point circle this holiday tree skirt. Scalloped edges provide a nice contrast to the points and angles of the stars as they fall softly around your Christmas tree. The simple design of the traditional patchwork blocks makes this tree skirt work nicely in any sort of decor, but it looks especially at home in a country-style setting. Once you've made one for under your tree, don't be surprised if friends start dropping hints that they'd like one too.

Skill Level: Intermediate

Size: Finished skirt is approximately 41 inches in diameter
Finished block is 7 inches square

Fabrics and Supplies

- ✓ 1½ yards of dark green print fabric for background and patchwork
- ✓ 1¼ yards of dark red print fabric for patchwork, binding, and scallops
- ✓ ⅓ yard of cream print fabric for patchwork
- ✓ 1¼ yards of fabric for quilt back
- ✓ Crib-size quilt batting (45 × 60 inches)
- ✓ Rotary cutter, ruler, and mat
- ✓ Template plastic

Cutting

All measurements include a ¼-inch seam allowance. The instructions are written for quick-cutting the A, B, C, and D pieces with a rotary cutter and ruler. Cut all strips across the fabric width. Make templates for pieces X, Y, and Z, using the patterns on pages 143–145. Mark the X and Y pieces with the right side of the template facing you. Turn the templates over so the wrong side is facing you to mark the reverse X and Y pieces.

You may want to cut just enough pieces to make one block to test your cutting and seam allowances for accuracy. If your finished block does not measure the size stated above, you can make adjustments before cutting all your fabric.

For easier piecing, use a large needle to pierce a hole through the X template at the point marked with a dot on the pattern. As you mark the X pieces for cutting, insert a pencil through the hole to make a dot on the fabric, indicating the ending point for that set-in seam.

From the dark green print fabric, cut:
- 8 X and 8 X reverse pieces
- 8 Y and 8 Y reverse pieces

- 8 C squares
  Cut one 4-inch strip. Cut 4-inch squares from the strip.

From the dark red print fabric, cut:
- 64 A triangles
  Cut two 2⅝-inch strips. From the strips, cut 32 squares, each 2⅝ inches square. Cut each square in half diagonally to make two triangles.
- One 18-inch square for bias binding
- 8 Z scallops

From the cream print fabric, cut:
- 32 B triangles
  Cut one 4¾-inch strip. From the strip, cut eight 4¾-inch squares. Cut each square in half diagonally in both directions to make four triangles.
- 32 D squares
  Cut two 2¼-inch strips. Cut 2¼-inch squares from the strips.

Piecing the Star Blocks

1. Referring to the **Fabric Key**, sew pairs of red A triangles to cream B triangles as shown in **Diagram 1**. Press the seam allowances toward the A triangles. Make 32 A/B units.

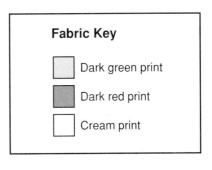

Diagram 1

2. Sew an A/B unit to the top and bottom of each green C square to make the middle rows of the blocks. Press the seam allowances toward the C squares.

3. Sew D squares to the ends of the remaining A/B units as shown in **Diagram 2** to make the side rows. Press seams toward the D squares.

Diagram 2

4. Join the rows as shown in **Diagram 3** to complete eight Sawtooth Star blocks. Press seam allowances toward the center row.

Make 8

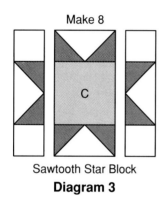

Sawtooth Star Block
Diagram 3

Making the Wedges and Assembling the Tree Skirt Top

1. Sew green Y and Y reverse pieces to two adjacent sides of a completed star block as shown in **Diagram 4**. Press the seam allowances toward the Y pieces.

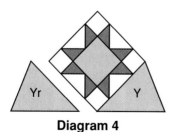

Diagram 4

2. Sew green X and X reverse pieces to the other two sides of the star block, referring to **Diagram 5**. Stop stitching at the dot marked on the seam allowance. Align raw edges of the

remaining short sides of the X pieces. Starting at the dots, sew the seam to the outer edge to join the X and X reverse pieces. Press seam allowances toward the X pieces.

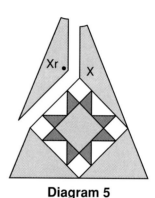

Diagram 5

3. Sew a red Z scallop to the bottom edge of the tree skirt wedge, referring to **Diagram 6.** Press seam allowances toward Z.

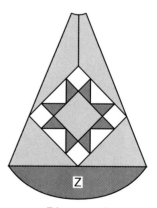

Diagram 6

4. Repeat to make a total of eight wedges. Join the wedges, leaving one seam unsewn for fitting around the tree trunk, as shown in the **Tree Skirt Diagram.** Press seam allowances to one side.

Quilting and Finishing

1. Mark quilting designs on tree skirt. The tree skirt pictured was machine quilted in the ditch around all pieces.

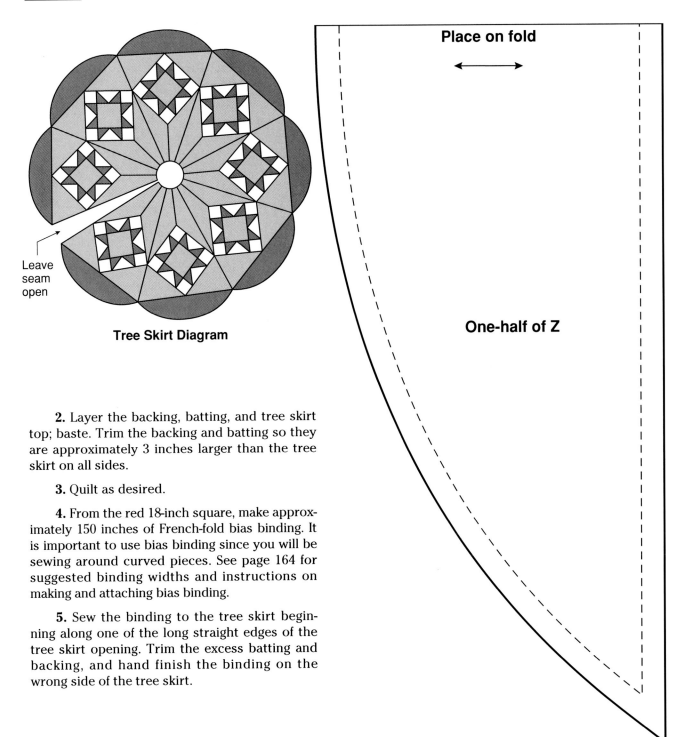

Tree Skirt Diagram

Leave seam open

Place on fold

One-half of Z

2. Layer the backing, batting, and tree skirt top; baste. Trim the backing and batting so they are approximately 3 inches larger than the tree skirt on all sides.

3. Quilt as desired.

4. From the red 18-inch square, make approximately 150 inches of French-fold bias binding. It is important to use bias binding since you will be sewing around curved pieces. See page 164 for suggested binding widths and instructions on making and attaching bias binding.

5. Sew the binding to the tree skirt beginning along one of the long straight edges of the tree skirt opening. Trim the excess batting and backing, and hand finish the binding on the wrong side of the tree skirt.

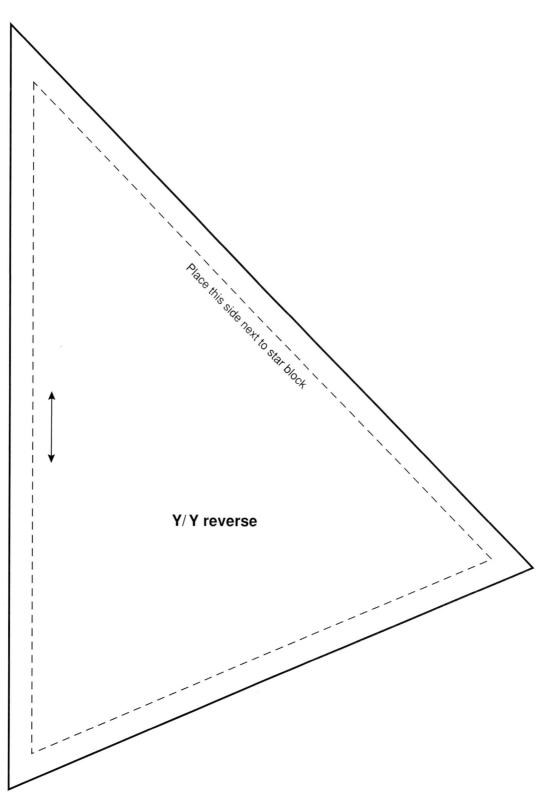

Place this side next to star block

Y/ Y reverse

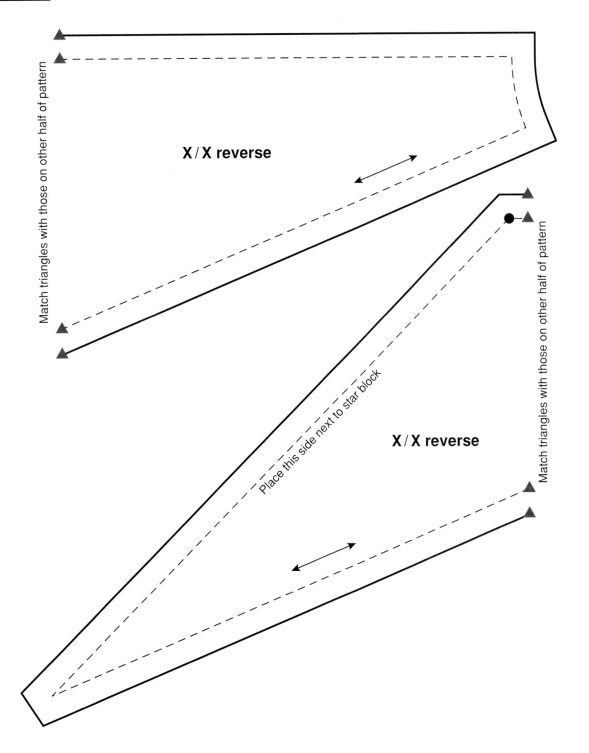

Match triangles with those on other half of pattern

X / X reverse

Place this side next to star block

X / X reverse

Match triangles with those on other half of pattern

Button Christmas Tree

Quiltmaker: Louy Danube

Search through your supply of scraps of gold trim and strings of
pearl beads to drape this delightful patchwork Christmas tree.
Then, raid your button box for buttons of all sizes to use as
ornaments and packages under it. As a final twinkling touch,
appliqué a gold lamé star with gold tinsel streaming from it in a
corner above the tree.

Skill Level: Intermediate

Size: Finished quilt is 29 inches square
Finished center tree section is 20 × 19 inches

Fabrics and Supplies

✓ ⅝ yard of beige print fabric for background

✓ ½ yard of blue floral print fabric for patchwork and binding

✓ ½ yard of green-and-gold print fabric for middle border and patchwork

✓ ⅓ yard of red paisley fabric for inner border and patchwork

✓ ⅓ yard of white print fabric for outer border

✓ ¼ yard of blue-and-black check fabric for outer border corners and patchwork

✓ ¼ yard of green paisley fabric for patchwork

✓ 2-inch gold lamé star appliqué

✓ Gold tinsel

✓ 1⅓ yards of ¼-inch blue-and-metallic-gold decorative trim

✓ 1⅓ yards of white pearl bead trim

✓ Approximately 90 buttons of gold, blue, white, and cream in assorted sizes

✓ Gold metallic thread for quilting

✓ 1 yard of fabric for quilt back

✓ Crib-size quilt batting (45 × 60 inches)

✓ Plastic-coated freezer paper

✓ Rotary cutter, ruler, and mat

✓ Scissors for cutting paper

Drawing the Master Pattern

Cut a 22-inch square of freezer paper. You may need to tape two pieces together to achieve the needed size. Draw a 20 × 19-inch rectangle on the paper. Draw a grid of 1-inch squares on the rectangle to use as a guide in enlarging the **Tree Pattern Diagram** on page 148. Draw the tree pattern, remembering that each square on the pattern equals one square inch. Please note that the pattern shapes are reversed from those in the photo on the opposite page. This is because you will be tracing onto the wrong side of the paper. When you cut out your pieces and press them onto your fabric, your shapes will match those in the photographed quilt. Label all tree shapes by color and row. The background pieces are labeled with a number for the Row and an L or R for left or right side for easier assembly. Cut apart the pattern on all drawn lines. Use the paper pieces as patterns to cut the fabric pieces. Discard the long paper strips that were above and below the tree.

If you prefer, you may enlarge the pattern by photocopying it at 400 percent of the original size. You will then need to trace your pattern onto the freezer paper, and cut apart the pieces as described above.

Cutting

Cut all borders using a rotary cutter and ruler. Measurements for the borders and the strips to sew to the top and bottom edges of the tree include ¼-inch seam allowances. Cut all strips across the fabric width. Measurements for borders are longer than needed; trim them to the exact length when they're added to the quilt top.

To use the freezer paper patterns to cut fabric pieces, use a dry iron on the wool setting. Press the shiny side of the freezer paper to the wrong side of the fabric, adhering the paper to the fabric. Space paper pieces at least ½ inch apart to allow for seam allowances. Use a rotary cutter and ruler to cut out the fabric pieces, adding ¼-inch seam allowances all around the pieces. Leave the paper attached to the fabric pieces until the tree is assembled.

From the beige print fabric, cut:
• One 2-inch strip. Cut this strip into two 20½-inch pieces for top and bottom background pieces.

• One 5-inch strip. From this strip cut background pieces 1L, 1R, 3L, and 3R.

• One 4-inch strip. From this strip cut background pieces 2L, 2R, 4L, and 4R.

From the blue floral print fabric, cut:
• 2 patchwork pieces for the tree

• Reserve the remaining fabric for binding

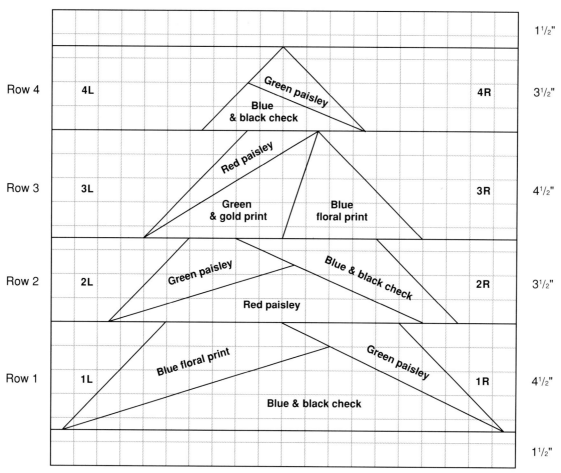

Enlarge pattern: 1 square = 1" or enlarge 400% on photocopy machine.

Tree Pattern Diagram

From the green-and-gold print fabric, cut:
- Four 3¼ × 30-inch middle border strips
- 1 patchwork piece for the tree

From the red paisley fabric, cut:
- Four 1¼ × 23-inch inner border strips
- 2 patchwork pieces for the tree

From the white print fabric, cut:
- Two 1½-inch side outer border strips
- Two 2-inch top and bottom outer border strips

From the blue-and-black check fabric, cut:
- Four 1½ × 2-inch rectangles for outer border corners
- 3 patchwork pieces for the tree

From the green paisley fabric, cut:
- 3 patchwork pieces for the tree

Piecing the Tree

1. Referring to the **Tree Pattern Diagram** and using the labels on your fabric pieces, reassemble the fabric pieces, using the paper patterns on the wrong side of the fabric to help you pin pieces together properly. As you join the pieces, stitch along the edges of the paper to insure accurate seams. For easiest piecing, sew pieces together in four rows. For each row, first join the tree pieces; then, add the background pieces. Press the seam allowances toward the darker fabric whenever possible.

2. Join the rows, then sew a beige background strip to the top and bottom of the tree. Press the seam allowances toward the bottom of the tree.

Adding the Borders

1. Fold each of the border strips for the inner and middle borders in half and crease them lightly to mark the border center. Center and sew a red paisley border to each green-and-gold print border. Press the seams toward the green borders.

2. Sew the inner and middle borders to the quilt top. Your border strips will be longer than your quilt length. *Do not cut off excess fabric.* The extra length is needed to miter the corners of the borders. Press the seams toward the borders. Miter the border corner seams, referring to page 160 for more detailed directions.

3. Measure the length and width of the quilt top by measuring through the center of the quilt. Trim the 2-inch white print border strips to the measurement of the quilt width (approximately 27½ inches long). Trim the 1½-inch white print borders to the measurement of the quilt length (approximately 26½ inches long).

4. Sew the 1½-inch side borders to the quilt top. Press the seam allowances toward the white print borders.

5. Sew a blue-and-black check corner rectangle to each end of the remaining 2-inch borders. Press the seam allowances toward the borders. Sew the borders to the top and bottom edges of the quilt top. Press the seam allowances toward the borders.

Quilting and Finishing

1. Mark quilting designs on the quilt top. The **Double Star Quilting Design** on this page was used for the green middle border and for the beige background around the tree.

2. Layer the backing, batting, and quilt top; baste. Trim the backing and batting so they are 3 inches larger than the quilt top.

3. Quilt all marked designs. Outline quilt around the tree and along the border seams, using gold metallic thread.

4. Make approximately 130 inches of blue floral French-fold binding. See page 164 for instructions on making and attaching binding.

5. Sew the binding to the quilt top. Trim excess batting and backing, and hand finish the binding to the back of the quilt. See page 167 for instructions for making a hanging sleeve.

Decorating the Tree

1. Referring to the photo on page 146, stitch pieces of trim to the tree. Cut lengths of pearl bead trim and hand stitch to the tree. Stitch buttons to the tree to look like ornaments. Cluster some buttons under the tree and stitch in place.

2. Tack a gold lamé star near the top right corner, using gold metallic thread at the inner points of the star. Attach gold tinsel below one point of the star, using the gold thread.

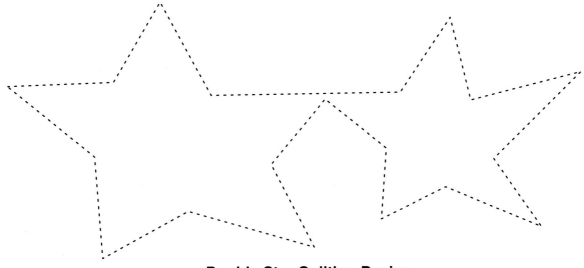

Double Star Quilting Design

Tips and Techniques

In this chapter you'll find detailed descriptions of general quiltmaking techniques, as well as hints and tips designed to make your quiltmaking successful and fun.

Supplies to Have on Hand

"Quiltmaking Basics" below describes the supplies you'll need to get started on the projects in this book. "Quiltmaking Time-Savers" describes quilting tools that you may want to work with. A few of the projects also require specialized supplies; those supplies are listed with the projects.

Quiltmaking Basics

- **Needles.** Use *sharps* for hand sewing and appliqué and *betweens* for hand quilting. For both sharps and betweens, the larger the number, the smaller the needle. The general rule is to start with the larger-size needles and move to smaller ones as you gain experience. Experiment with different sizes to see which are most comfortable in your hand and the easiest to manipulate through the fabric.
- **Straight pins.** Do not use pins that have become burred or rusted; they may leave marks in your fabric. Long (1½-inch) pins with glass or plastic heads are easy to work with, especially when pinning layers.
- **Scissors.** If you are cutting your fabric with scissors, use a good, sharp pair of dressmaker's shears. Use these only on fabric. You should also have a pair of

small, sharp embroidery scissors for trimming threads and seam allowances, and a pair of general scissors for cutting paper and template plastic.
- **Iron and ironing board.** Careful pressing is important for accurate piecing. To save steps and increase efficiency, keep your ironing board and iron close to your sewing area.
- **Sewing machine.** Keep it clean, oiled, and in good working order.
- **Template plastic or cardboard.** Templates are rigid master patterns used to mark patchwork and appliqué shapes on fabric. Thin, semitransparent plastic, available in sheets at quilt and craft shops, is ideal, although poster-weight cardboard can also be used for templates.
- **Thread.** Always use good-quality thread. For sewing, use either 100 percent cotton or cotton-covered polyester. For quilting, use special quilting thread.

Quiltmaking Time-Savers

- **Rotary cutter and cutting mat.** For greater speed and accuracy, you can cut all border strips and many other pieces with a rotary cutter instead of scissors. You must always use a specially designed cutting mat when working with a rotary cutter. The self-healing surface of the mat protects the work surface and helps to grip the fabric to keep it from slipping. An all-purpose cutting mat size is 18 × 24 inches. See the section on rotary cutting on

page 152 for tips on using the cutter.
- **See-through ruler.** The companion to the rotary cutter and mat is the see-through plastic ruler. It comes in several sizes and shapes; a useful size to have on hand is a 6 × 24 inch heavy-duty ruler that is marked in inches, quarter-inches, and eighth-inches and has a 45 degree angle line for mitering. Also handy are a ruled plastic square, 12 × 12 inches or larger, and a 6 × 12 inch ruler for cutting segments from strip sets.
- **Plastic-coated freezer paper.** Quilters have discovered many handy uses for this type of paper, which is stocked in grocery stores with other food-wrapping supplies. Choose a quality brand, such as Reynolds.

About Fabric

Since fabric is the most essential element in a quilt, what you buy and how you treat it are important considerations. Buy the best that you can afford; you'll be far happier with the results if you work with good-quality materials. Read through this section for additional tips on selecting and preparing fabric.

Selecting Fabrics

The instructions for each of the quilts in this book include the amount of fabric you will need. When choosing fabrics, most experienced quilters insist on 100 percent cotton broadcloth, or dress-weight, fabric. It presses well and handles easily, whether you are sewing by hand or machine.

If there is a quilt specialty shop in your area, the sales staff there can help you choose fabrics. Most home-sewing stores also have a section of all-cotton fabrics for quilters. If you have scraps left over from other sewing, use them only if they are all-cotton and all of similar weight.

Gaining Color Confidence

Deciding on a color scheme and choosing the fabrics can seem daunting to a beginner. You can take some of the mystery out of the process by learning the basics of color theory. Consult books on color theory, or seek out a class at a local quilt shop or quilt conference. Learn how helpful a color wheel can be, and understand the importance of value (the lightness or darkness of a color) and scale (the size of the print). Your color confidence will grow as you learn the basics and then experiment with different combinations.

Purchasing Fabrics

The yardages given for projects in this book are based on 44- to 45-inch-wide fabrics. These yardages are adequate for both the template and rotary-cutting methods. They have been double-checked for accuracy and always include a little extra. Be aware, however, that fabric is sometimes narrower than the size listed on the bolt, and that any quilter, no matter how experienced, can make a mistake in cutting. It never hurts to buy an extra half-yard of the fabrics for your quilt, just to be safe.

Preparing Fabrics

For best results, prewash, dry, and press your fabrics before using them in your quilts.

Prewashing allows shrinkage to occur and removes finishes and sizing, softening the cloth and making it easier to handle. Washing also allows colors to bleed before light and dark fabrics are combined in a quilt. If one of your fabrics bleeds, set the dye by soaking the whole piece of fabric in a solution of three parts cold water to one part vinegar. Rinse the fabric two or three times in warm water. If the fabric still bleeds, don't use it in your quilt.

Keep in mind that prewashing might remove the lovely finish from chintz and polished cotton. If you want to use these fabrics to add sparkle to your quilts, save them for wallhangings or other items that won't need to be laundered.

SNIP CORNERS

Before putting your fabric in the washer, snip a ½-inch triangle off the four corners of each piece of yardage. The snips will prevent your fabric from raveling in the washer and dryer. ❖

To prewash, use your automatic washer, warm water, and a mild detergent. Dry fabric on a medium setting in your dryer or outdoors on a clothesline. It's a good idea to get in the habit of washing all your fabrics as soon as you bring them home, even if you're not planning to use them right away. Then, when you are ready to use a fabric, you won't have to wonder whether it's been washed.

While prewashing is best, some quilters prefer the crispness of unwashed fabric and feel

they can achieve more accurate machine-sewn patchwork by using fabric right off the bolt. Some machine quilters like to use unwashed fabric, then wash the project after quilting and binding so the quilt looks crinkled and old-fashioned. The risk in washing after stitching is that colors may bleed.

Cutting the Fabric

For each project in this book, the cutting instructions follow the list of fabrics and supplies. To make the book as easy to use as possible, the cutting instructions appear two ways. Quilters who prefer the traditional method of making templates and scissor-cutting individual pieces will find full-size patterns or template sizes and cutting guidelines. For quilters who prefer to rotary cut, quick-cutting directions speed things along. You may want to try a combination of techniques, using scissors and templates for pattern pieces and the rotary cutter for straight pieces like the borders and bindings. Experiment and see which techniques work best for you.

For some of the projects there are no patterns. In these cases, you will either measure and cut squares, triangles, and rectangles directly from the fabric, or you will be instructed to sew strips together into strip sets and then cut them into special units to combine with others.

Although rotary cutting can be faster and more accurate than cutting with scissors, it does have one disadvantage: It does not always result in the most efficient use of fabric. In some cases, the quick-cutting method featured in the project will result in long strips of leftover fabric. Don't think of these as wasted bits of fabric; just add these strips to your scrap bag for future projects.

KEEP PATCHES ORGANIZED

Some quilts require hundreds, or thousands, of patchwork pieces. A favorite grocery store item of many quilters is a box of "zipper"-type sandwich or freezer bags. Stacks of like fabric pieces stay well organized, and the zipper closures keep dust off of your fabric. ❖

Tips on Rotary Cutting

- Keep the rotary cutter out of children's reach. The blade is extremely sharp!
- Make it a habit to slide the blade guard into place as soon as you stop cutting.
- Always cut *away* from yourself.
- Square off the end of your fabric before measuring and cutting pieces, as shown in **Diagram 1.** Place a ruled square or right-angle triangle on the fold, and place a 6 × 24-inch ruler against the side of the square. Hold the ruler in place, remove the square, and cut along the edge of the ruler. If you are left-handed, work from the other end of the fabric.
- Use the right cutter for the job. The large size is best for cutting several layers. The small cutter is ideal for cutting around thick plastic templates since it is easier to control around curves and points.

6" X 24" ruler

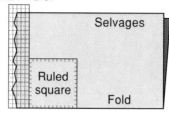

Diagram 1: Square off the uneven edges of the fabric before cutting the strips.

- When cutting strips or rectangles, cut on the crosswise grain, as shown in **Diagram 2,** unless instructed otherwise. Strips can then be cut into squares, as shown. You can stack two or three folded strips on top of each other so you have four or six layers of fabric, and you will be cutting squares from all the strips at once.

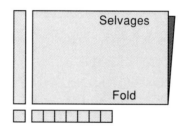

Diagram 2: Cut strips or rectangles on the crosswise grain. Cut the strips into squares.

- Check strips periodically to make sure the fabric is square and the strips are straight, not angled. (See **Diagram 3.**) If your strips are not straight, refold the fabric making sure the selvages are even, square off the edge, and cut again.
- Cut triangles from squares, as shown in **Diagram 4.** The project directions will tell you whether to cut the square into two triangles by making one diagonal cut (**Diagram 4A**) or into four

triangles by making two diagonal cuts (**4B**).

Diagram 3: Check to see that the strips are straight. If they are angled, refold the fabric and square off the edge again.

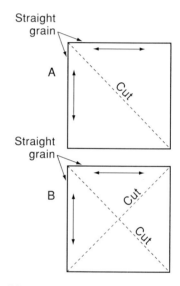

Diagram 4: Cut two triangles from a square by making one diagonal cut (A). Cut four triangles from a square by making two diagonal cuts (B).

OIL CHANGE FOR EXTRA MILEAGE

Maintain your rotary cutter for maximum cutting ease. If the wheel seems sluggish, remove the nut that holds the blade and place a drop of sewing machine oil on the blade. Sometimes a blade that seems dull just needs a little lubrication. ❖

Making and Using Templates

The patterns in this book are printed full size, with no drafting required. For some of the pieced projects, you will have the option of either making templates using the patterns or dimensions given and cutting fabric pieces individually, or using a rotary cutter to quick-cut them.

Thin, semitransparent plastic makes excellent, durable templates. Lay the plastic over the book page, carefully trace the patterns onto the plastic, and cut them out with scissors. To make cardboard templates, transfer the patterns to tracing paper, glue the paper to the cardboard, and cut out the templates. Copy identification letters and any grain line instructions onto your templates. Always check your templates against the printed pattern for accuracy.

The patchwork patterns in the book are printed with double lines: an inner dashed line and an outer solid line. If you intend to sew your patchwork by hand, trace the inner dashed line to make finished-size templates. Cut out the templates on the traced line. Draw around the template on the wrong side of the fabric, as shown in **Diagram 5,** leaving ½ inch between lines. The lines you draw are the sewing lines. Then mark the ¼-inch seam allowances before you cut out the fabric pieces.

If you plan to sew your patchwork by machine, use the outer solid line and make your templates with seam allowances included. Draw around the templates on the wrong side of the

fabric, as shown in **Diagram 6.** The line you draw is the cutting line. Sew with an exact ¼-inch seam for perfect patchwork.

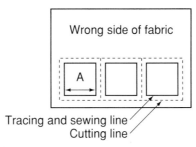

Diagram 5: *If piecing by hand, mark around the template on the wrong side of the fabric. Cut it out, adding ¼-inch seam allowances on all sides.*

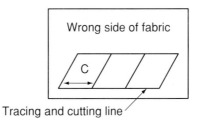

Diagram 6: *If piecing by machine, use templates with seam allowances included.*

Patterns for appliqué pieces are printed with only a single line. Make finished-size templates for appliqué pieces. Draw around templates on the right side of the fabric, as shown in **Diagram 7,** leaving ½ inch between pieces. The lines you draw will be your fold-under lines, or guides for turning under the edges of the appliqué pieces. Then add scant ¼-inch seam allowances as you cut out the pieces.

Tips on Piecing

The standard seam allowance for piecing is ¼ inch. For precise patchwork, where the

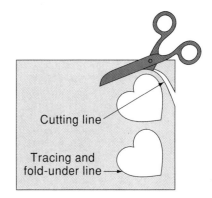

Diagram 7: *Draw around the templates on the right side of the fabric for appliqué pieces. Add seam allowances as you cut out the pieces.*

pieces always meet exactly where they should, you must be vigilant about accurate seam allowances. Some sewing machines come with a handy seam allowance guide marked alongside the feed dogs. On other machines, the distance from the needle to the outside of the presser foot is ¼ inch. (Measure your machine to be sure this is accurate.) On machines that have no built-in guides, you can create your own. Measure ¼-inch from the needle and lay down a 2-inch-long piece of masking tape. Continue to add layers of masking tape on top of the first one until you have a raised edge against which you can guide fabric, automatically measuring the ¼-inch seam allowance.

When assembling pieced blocks, keep in mind these basic rules: Combine smaller pieces to make larger units, join larger units into rows or sections, and join sections to complete the blocks. If you follow these rules, you should be able to build most blocks using only straight seams. Setting-in pieces at an angle should only be done when necessary. (Pointers appear on the opposite page.)

Lay out the pieces for the block with right sides up, as shown in the project diagram, before you sew. For quilts with multiple blocks, cut out and piece a sample block first to make sure your fabrics work well together and you have cut out the pieces accurately.

Hand Piecing

For hand piecing, use finished-size templates to cut your fabric pieces. Join the pieces by matching marked sewing lines and securing them with pins. Sew with a running stitch from seam line to seam line, as shown in **Diagram 8,** rather than from raw edge to raw edge. As you sew, check to see that your stitching is staying on the lines, and make a backstitch every four or five stitches to reinforce and strengthen the seam. Secure the corners with an extra backstitch.

Diagram 8: *Join the pieces with a running stitch, backstitching every four or five stitches.*

When you cross a seam allowance of previously joined smaller units, leave the seam allowance free rather than stitching it down. Make a backstitch just before you cross, slip the needle through the seam

allowance, make a backstitch after you cross, then resume stitching the seam. (See **Diagram 9.**) When your block is finished, press the seam allowances toward the darker fabrics.

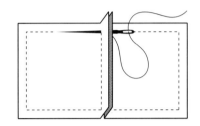

Diagram 9: *When hand piecing, leave the seam allowances free by slipping through without stitching them down.*

Machine Piecing

For machine piecing, cut the fabric pieces using templates with seam allowances included or use a rotary cutter to quick-cut. Before sewing a block, sew a test seam to make sure you are taking accurate $\frac{1}{4}$-inch seams. Even $\frac{1}{16}$ inch of inaccuracy can result in a block that is not the right size. Adjust your machine to sew 10 to 12 stitches per inch. Select a neutral-color thread such as a medium gray that blends well with the fabrics you are using.

Join the pieces by sewing from raw edge to raw edge. Press the seams before crossing them with other seams. Since the seam allowances will be stitched down when crossed with another seam, you'll need to think about the direction in which you want them to lie. Press the seam allowances toward darker fabrics whenever possible to prevent them from shadowing through lighter ones. For more information on pressing, see page 156.

When you join blocks into rows, press all the seam allowances in opposite directions from row to row. Then, when you join the rows, abut the pressed seam allowances to produce precise intersections.

In many quilts, you need to sew a large number of the same size or shape pieces together to create units for the blocks. For a bed-size quilt, this can mean a hundred or more squares, triangles, or rectangles that need to be stitched together. A timesaving method known as assembly-line piecing can reduce the drudgery. Run pairs of pieces or units through the sewing machine one after another without cutting the thread, as shown in **Diagram 10.** Once all the units you need have been sewn, snip them apart and press. You can continue to add on more pieces to these units, assembly-line fashion, until the sections are the size you need.

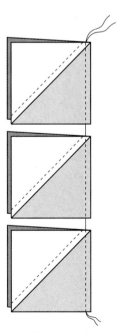

Diagram 10: *Feed the units through the machine without cutting the thread.*

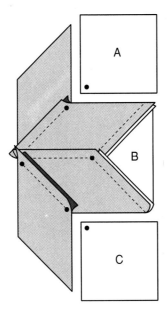

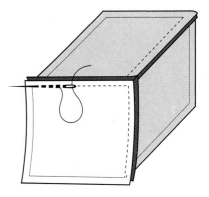

Diagram 13: Pin the adjacent edge to the other side of the angle and stitch from the corner to the outside.

EXTRA BOBBINS

When you settle in for a full day of sewing patchwork, wind two or three extra bobbins of your neutral thread and keep them handy. You'll be inconvenienced less if you only need to replace an empty bobbin instead of unthreading your machine to wind a new one. ❖

Setting-In Pieces

Not all patchwork patterns can be assembled with continuous straight seams. An example is the California Star quilt on page 72. Background pieces must be set into the angled openings created by the diamonds. Setting-in calls for precise stitching as you insert pieces into angles, as shown in **Diagram 11.** In this example, pieces A, B, and C are set into the angles created by the four joined diamond pieces.

Setting-In by Hand

Setting-in by hand is simple. Following the directions on page 153, make finished-size templates. Trace around the templates, then mark the ¼-inch seam allowances before you cut out the pieces.

1. Pin piece to be set in to one side of angle, right sides together, matching corners exactly.

2. Starting ¼ inch from the outside edge and working to the corner, stitch along the marked seam line, as shown in **Diagram 12,** removing pins as you go. Stop ¼ inch from the inside corner, at your marked seam line. Knot the thread and clip it.

Diagram 11: Setting-in calls for careful matching of points and precise stitching. Here, pieces A, B, and C are set into the angles created by the four joined diamonds.

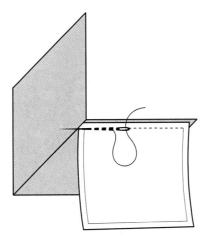

Diagram 12: Pin the pieces right sides together and stitch from the outside into the corner.

3. Bring the adjacent edge up and pin it to the other side of the angle, as shown in **Diagram 13.** Hand stitch the seam from the corner out, stopping ¼ inch from the edge at the end of the marked seam line.

Setting-In by Machine

If you are setting-in pieces by machine, make special templates that will allow you to mark dots on the fabric at the points where pieces will come together. By matching dots on the pattern pieces as they meet at the angle, you can be sure of a smooth fit. To make these templates, first mark the sewing lines, then use a large needle to pierce a hole at each setting-in point. (See **Diagram 14.**) As you trace the templates onto the wrong side of the fabric, push the tip of the pencil through each of these holes to create a dot. Mark all corners of each pattern piece. You may discover later that you want to turn the piece to adjust color or pattern placement; marking all the corners allows you that option.

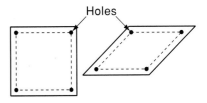

Diagram 14: For setting-in pieces by machine, make templates with holes at the setting-in points.

1. Pin a piece to one side of the angle with right sides together, matching the dots. Beginning and ending the seam with a backstitch, sew from the raw edge into the corner, and stop the stitching exactly on the marked corner dot. Don't allow any stitching to extend into the seam allowance. (See **Diagram 15.**)

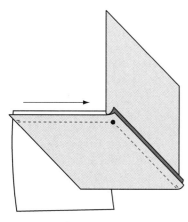

Diagram 15: Pin the piece to one side of the angle, matching dots. Stitch from the edge into the corner.

2. Remove the work from your sewing machine to realign the pieces for the other side of the seam. Swing the other side of the angled piece up, match the dots, and pin the pieces together.

3. Sew from the corner dot to the outside edge to complete the seam, again backstitching at the beginning and end. (See **Diagram 16.**) Press the seams toward the set-in piece.

Pressing Basics

Proper pressing can make a big difference in the appearance of a finished block or quilt top. Quilters are divided on the issue of whether a steam or dry iron is best. Experiment to see

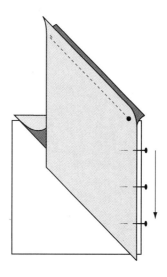

Diagram 16: Matching dots, pin the piece to the other side of the angle. Stitch from the corner dot to the outside edge.

IRON IN REVERSE

The tapered end of a standard ironing board is designed for pressing garments. Many quilters turn their ironing board around, keeping the tapered end at their right if they're right-handed. The narrow end provides plenty of room for resting the iron, and the wider, squared-off end allows more surface area for pressing large quilt tops. ❖

which works best for you. For each project, pressing instructions are given as needed in the step-by-step directions. Review the list of guidelines that follow to brush up on your general pressing techniques.

• Press a seam before crossing it with another seam.

• Press seam allowances to one side, not open.

• Press seams of adjacent rows of blocks, or rows within blocks, in opposite directions so the pressed seams will abut as the rows are joined. (See **Diagram 17.**)

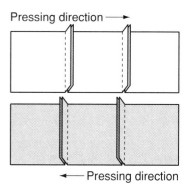

Pressing direction ⟶

⟵ Pressing direction

Diagram 17: Press the seams of adjacent rows in opposite directions. When the rows are placed right sides together to be joined, the pressed seams will abut.

• If possible, press seams toward darker fabrics to avoid show-through on the front of the quilt.

• Press, don't iron. Bring the iron down gently and firmly on the fabric from above, rather than rub the iron over the patchwork.

• Avoid pressing appliqués on the right side after they have been stitched to the background fabric. They are prettiest when slightly puffed, rather than flat. To press appliqués, turn the piece over and press very gently on the back side of the background fabric.

Hand Appliqué

Several of the quilts in this book include beautiful appliqué. The true tests of fine appliqué work are smoothly turned, crisp edges and sharp points; no unsightly bumps or gaps; and nearly invisible stitches.

Depending on your personal preference, there are three popular techniques that can help you achieve flawless appliqué. Each of these methods is described in detail below.

For any of these methods, use thread that matches the appliqué pieces, and stitch the appliqués to the background fabric with a blind hem or appliqué stitch, as shown in **Diagram 18.** Invest in a package of long, thin size 11 or 12 needles marked sharps. Make stitches ⅛ inch apart or closer, and keep them snug.

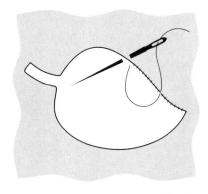

Diagram 18: Stitch the appliqués to the background with a blind hem stitch. The stitches should be nearly invisible.

When constructing appliqué blocks, always work from background to foreground. When an appliqué piece will be covered or overlapped by another, stitch the underneath piece to the background fabric first.

Basting-Back Method

1. Make finished-size cardboard or thin plastic templates. Mark around the templates on the right side of the fabric to draw fold-under lines. Draw lightly so the lines are thin.

2. Cut out the pieces a scant ¼ inch to the outside of the marked lines.

3. For each appliqué piece, turn the seam allowance under, folding along the marked line, and baste close to the fold with white or natural thread. Clip concave curves and clefts before basting. (See **Diagram 19.**) Do not baste back edges that will be covered by another appliqué.

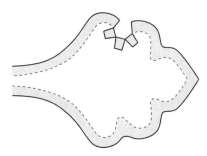

Diagram 19: Clip any concave curves, then baste back the seam allowances.

4. Pin the appliqués in place and stitch them to the background fabric. Remove the basting after the pieces are stitched down.

Freezer Paper Method

1. Make finished-size plastic templates for appliqué patterns.

2. Place templates on the smooth (not shiny) side of the freezer paper and draw around them. Do not add seam allowances. Cut out the patterns along the lines. Make a separate pattern for each appliqué piece. For example, in the Christmas Rose quilt (page 132), you need to draw four A leaves, one B flower, and five C flowers.

TOOTHPICK TURNING

Some quilters like the results they get with needle-turn appliqué, but they find that using a needle to turn their fabric can sometimes be slippery business. For easier turning under of your fabric edge, keep a wooden toothpick handy. Instead of using the tip of the needle to turn your edge under, use the tip of the toothpick. The rougher surface of the wood will keep your fabric from slipping. ❖

3. Using a dry iron set on wool, press the paper patterns to the proper fabric, placing the shiny side of the paper on the right side of the fabric. Leave about ½ inch between pieces for seam allowances.

4. Cut out the appliqués ⅛ inch to the outside of the paper edge to allow for seams. Leave the paper attached to the fabric.

5. Pin the appliqué in place on the background fabric with the paper still attached. As you stitch the appliqué to the background, turn under the seam allowance along the edge of the freezer paper, aligning the fold of the fabric with the paper edge. Once the piece is stitched down completely, gently peel off the paper pattern.

Needle-Turn Method

1. Use plastic or cardboard templates to mark finished-size pieces. Mark lightly on the right side of the fabric.

2. Cut out the pieces a generous ⅛ inch larger than the finished size.

3. Pin the pieces in position on the background fabric. Use the tip and shank of your appliqué needle to turn under ½-inch-long sections of seam allowance at a time. As you turn under a section, press it flat with your thumb and then stitch it in place.

Making Bias Strips for Stems and Vines

Fabric strips cut on the bias have more give and are easier to manipulate than strips cut on the straight grain. This makes them ideal for creating beautiful curving stems and vines and twisting ribbons. Bias strips enhance several of the projects in this book, including the Fantasy Remembered wallhanging (page 78). The quilt instructions include directions for cutting bias strips the proper width.

Cut bias strips with your rotary cutter using the 45 degree angle line on your see-through ruler. Straighten the left edge of your fabric as described on page 152. Align the 45 degree angle line on your see-through ruler with the bottom edge of the fabric, as shown in **Diagram 20A,** and cut along the edge of the ruler to trim off the corner. Move the ruler across the fabric, cutting parallel strips in the needed width, as shown in **20B.** Once the strips are cut, prepare them for appliqué by using a bias bar as described below.

Narrow bias strips for appliqué can be made using metal or plastic bars called bias bars or Celtic bars. You'll need this type of tool for making the Bringing Lilies to the Table quilt

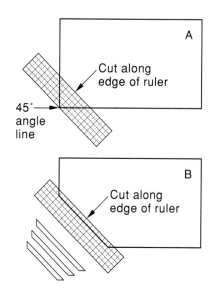

Diagram 20: Use the 45 degree angle line on your see-through ruler to trim off the corner of the fabric (A). Then move the ruler across the fabric, cutting parallel strips of the width needed (B).

(page 35) and Fantasy Remembered wallhanging (page 78). Bias bars are available in quilt shops and through mail-order catalogs. The bar should be equal to the required finished width of the bias strip. Cut a fabric strip wide enough to wrap around the bar and to allow for the ⅛-inch seam allowances. Fold the strip in half lengthwise, wrong sides facing, and using a ⅛-inch seam allowance, sew the long raw edges of the strip together. Insert the bar into the tube. Center the seam along the bar and press, as shown in **Diagram 21.** Continue to slide the bar along the tube, pressing as you go. Remove the bar and press the strip one more time.

Machine Appliqué

Machine appliqué is ideal for decorative accessories like the

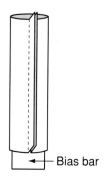

Diagram 21: Slip bias bar into fabric tube. Center seam along top of bar and press.

Duck Quilt (page 42). It's a quick-and-easy way to add appliqué pieces to projects that you don't want to spend time hand stitching. Plus, machine appliqué stands up well to repeated washings, so it's great for place mats and clothing.

Satin stitch machine appliqué can be done on any sewing machine that has a zigzag stitch setting. Use a zigzag presser foot with a channel on the bottom that will allow the heavy ridge of stitching to feed evenly. Match your thread to the appliqué pieces. Set your machine for a medium-width zigzag stitch and a very short stitch length. Test stitch on a scrap of fabric. The stitches should form a band of color and be ⅛ to ³⁄₁₆ inch wide. If necessary, loosen the top tension slightly so that the top thread is barely pulled to the wrong side.

1. To prepare the appliqué pieces, use Wonder-Under or a similar paper-backed fusible webbing, following the manufacturer's instructions. For most products, the procedure is the same: Trace the appliqué shapes onto the paper side of the webbing and roughly cut out the designs, as shown in **Diagram 22.**

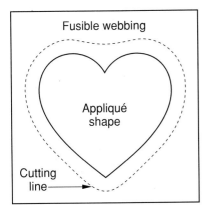

Diagram 22: Trace the appliqué shape onto the paper side of the webbing and roughly cut out the design.

2. Using a dry iron set on Wool, fuse the webbing onto the wrong side of the fabrics you have chosen for appliqués. Cut out the pieces along the tracing lines, as shown in **Diagram 23,** allowing approximately ¼-inch underlap on adjacent pieces within a design. Peel off the paper backing, position the pieces on the background fabric, and fuse in place.

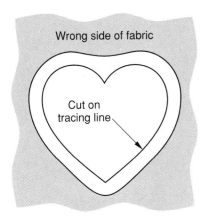

Diagram 23: Fuse the webbing onto the wrong side of the fabric and cut along the tracing line.

3. Stabilize the background fabric by pinning a sheet of typing paper or commercial stabilizer such as Tear-Away to the wrong side of the background fabric in the areas where you will be stitching. Some quilters like to use freezer paper as a stabilizer for machine appliqué.

4. Machine satin stitch around the edges of the appliqué pieces, covering the raw edges. Change thread colors to match the pieces. When stitching is complete, carefully tear away the stabilizer from the wrong side.

Assembling Quilt Tops

To assemble a quilt comprised of rows of blocks, such as Moon and Stars (page 85), refer to the quilt diagram or photograph and lay out all the pieced or appliqué blocks, plain blocks, and setting pieces right side up, positioned as they will be in the finished quilt.

Pin and sew all the blocks together in vertical or horizontal rows for straight-set quilts and in diagonal rows for diagonal-set quilts. Press the seams in opposite directions from row to row. Join the rows, abutting the pressed seam allowances so the intersections will be accurate.

To keep a large quilt top manageable, join rows into pairs first and then join the pairs, rather than add each row to an increasingly unwieldy top.

When pressing a completed top, press on the back side first, carefully clipping and removing hanging threads; then press the front, making sure all the seams are flat.

Tips for Successful Borders

For most of the quilts in this book, directions for adding the appropriate borders are included with the instructions for that quilt. Here are some general tips that can help you with any quilt you make.

- Cut borders to the desired finished width plus ½ inch for seam allowances. Always cut border strips several inches longer than needed, just to be safe. (Cutting instructions for borders in this book already include seam allowances and extra length.)

- Before adding borders, measure your completed inner quilt top. Measure through the center of the quilt rather than along the edges, which may have stretched from handling. Use this measurement to determine the exact length of your borders. This is an important step; if you don't measure first and simply give the edge of the quilt as much border as it "wants," you may end up with rippled edges on your quilt. Measuring and marking your borders first will allow you to make any necessary adjustment or ease in any fabric that may have stretched along the edge.

- Measure and mark sewing dimensions on the ends of borders before sewing them on, and wait to trim off excess fabric until after sewing.

- Fold border strips in half crosswise and press lightly or mark with a pin to indicate the halfway mark. Align this mark with the center point along the quilt side when pinning on the border.

- Press border seam allowances away from the center of the quilt.

Mitered Borders

Mitered borders add a professional touch to your quilt and are not hard to master if you keep in mind a few basics.

1. Start by measuring your finished quilt top through the center to determine the length the borders should be.

2. If you have multiple borders that are to be mitered, find and mark the center of each border strip. Match the centers, sew the strips together, and treat them as one unit.

3. With a ruler and pencil, mark a ¼-inch sewing line along one long edge of the border strip. For a multiple border, mark the inner strip that goes next to the quilt. Fold the strip in half crosswise and press lightly to mark the halfway point.

4. Starting at the halfway point, measure out in each direction to one-half of the desired finished border length, and make a mark on the sewing line.

5. Use a ruler that has a 45 degree angle line to mark the miter sewing line. Referring to **Diagram 24,** draw a line from the end mark made in Step 4 to the outer edge of the border strip. Mark a cutting line ¼ inch to the outside of the sewing line, but don't trim until after the border is sewn to the quilt top.

6. Pin the marked border strip to the quilt top, matching the crease at the halfway point to the center side of the quilt. Position the end marks on the border strip ¼ inch in from the raw edges of the quilt top. Pin the border to the quilt top, distributing any fullness evenly along the length of the border. Repeat for all remaining border strips.

7. Stitch the borders to the quilt top, starting and stopping at the end marks exactly ¼ inch from each end. Backstitch to secure the stitching. Press the seam allowances away from the quilt top.

8. Sew the miters by folding the quilt diagonally, right sides together, and aligning the marked miter lines on adjacent borders. Stitch from the inner corner mark all the way to the outer raw edge.

9. Check the accuracy of your miter, then trim the excess seam allowance.

Quilting Designs

Exquisite quilting is often the element that makes a quilt truly special. Even a simple quilt can be set apart by the fine workmanship demonstrated by small, even stitches. While some quilts lend themselves to very simple quilting patterns, such as outline quilting, others are beautifully accented by cables, feathers, and floral designs. Suggestions for quilting designs are included with many of the project instructions. You can duplicate the design the quiltmaker used, create your own, or choose one of the many quilting templates available at quilt shops and through mail-order catalogs.

MAKE YOUR OWN STENCILS

To make a stencil or template for marking quilting designs on dark fabric, trace the pattern from the book onto semitransparent template plastic. Cut out the template along the outer edge. For the inner design, use a large darning needle to poke holes approximately ½ inch apart along the traced lines. Use a marking pencil to mark dots through the holes onto your fabric. For easier poking and neater holes, heat the darning needle to slightly melt the plastic. Be sure to use an insulated pliers to hold your hot needle. ❖

Some quilting needs no design template. Outline quilting simply follows the seams of the patchwork. It can be in the ditch, that is, right next to the seam, or ¼ inch away from the seam. In-the-ditch quilting needs no marking. For ¼-inch outline quilting, you can work by eye or use ¼-inch-wide masking tape as a guide for stitching. These and other straight lines can also be marked lightly with a pencil and ruler.

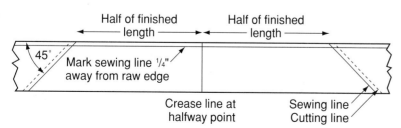

Diagram 24: Mark the border strips for mitering before sewing them to the quilt top.

Another type of quilting that needs no marking is called echo quilting. Look at the photo of Great-Grandma Goebel's Bridal Quilt (page 28) for a beautiful example of this type of quilting. It consists of lines of quilting that outline appliqués in concentric rings or shapes. The lines are generally spaced about ½ inch apart.

In contrast to outline and echo quilting, which need no marking, quilting designs, such as the designs for Baskets of Love (page 16), should be marked before the quilt top is layered with batting and backing. How you mark depends on whether your fabric is light or dark.

Marking Light Fabrics

If your fabric is a light color that you can see through, such as muslin, you can place the pattern under the quilt top and easily trace the quilting design onto the fabric. First, either trace the design out of the book onto good-quality tracing paper or photocopy it. If necessary, darken the lines with a black permanent marker. If the pattern will be used many times, glue it to cardboard to make it sturdy. Place the pattern under the quilt top and carefully mark the designs on the fabric, making a thin, continuous line that will be covered by the quilting thread. Use a silver quilter's pencil or a mechanical pencil with thin (0.5 mm) medium (B) lead.

Marking Dark Fabrics

Use a white or silver pencil to mark quilting designs on dark fabrics. Mark from the top by drawing around a hard-edged quilting design template. To make simple templates, trace

the design onto template plastic and cut out around the outer edge. Then trace around the outer edge of the template onto the fabric, and add inner lines by eye.

You may be able to use the method described above (placing the pattern underneath the fabric) if you place the pattern and the fabric on a light box while marking. The light shining through the paper and fabric will allow you to see the pattern outline through even the darkest fabrics. Any glass-topped table makes an excellent light box area. Take the lamp shade off a small lamp and place the lamp under the table. Tape your pattern to the tabletop, place the fabric on top of the pattern, and trace the pattern onto the fabric.

Quilt Backings

For each of the projects in this book, the list of fabrics and supplies includes yardage for the quilt back. For wallhangings that are narrower than 44 inches, simply use a full width of yardage cut several inches longer than the quilt top. For the wider wallhangings and most of the bed quilts, the quilt backing must be pieced unless you purchase extrawide fabric, such as 90- or 108-inch-wide muslin.

Whenever possible, piece quilt backings in two or three panels with the seams running parallel to the long side of the quilt. Backs for quilts such as Midnight Starburst (page 98), which is narrower than 80 inches wide, can easily be pieced this way out of two lengths of yardage. Divide the yardage in half crosswise. Then, to avoid having a seam down the center of the quilt

back, divide one of the pieces in half lengthwise. Sew a narrow panel to each side of a full-width central panel, as shown in **Diagram 25.** Be sure to trim the selvages from the yardage before joining the panels. Press the seams away from the center of the quilt.

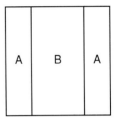

Diagram 25: Divide the yardage in half crosswise; divide one of the pieces in half lengthwise. Sew one of those halves to each side of the full-width piece, as shown.

For some quilts, you may make more sensible use of your yardage by piecing the back so that the seams run parallel to the short side of the quilt, as shown in **Diagram 26** on page 162. For example, Baskets of Love (page 16) is 84¾ × 113 inches. To have the seams run parallel to the long side of the quilt, you would need three 3½-yard-long panels, for a total of 10½ yards of fabric. However, if the seams run parallel to the short side of the quilt, you would need three panels, each approximately 2⅝ yards long, for a total of 7⅞ yards of fabric.

To prepare the backing, divide the yardage crosswise into three panels. Trim the selvages and sew the full-width panels together along their long sides. The finished quilt backing should look like the one shown in **Diagram 26.**

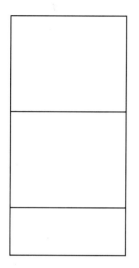

Diagram 26: Divide the yardage crosswise into three equal panels. Sew the three full-width panels together side by side. Layer the backing, batting, and quilt top with the seams running parallel to the short side of the quilt top, as shown. Trim the excess from one panel as needed.

Types of Quilt Batting

Quilters generally spend a lot of time selecting the fabrics for their quilts, but often not enough time choosing the batting they will use. When purchasing batting for your quilt, take the time to read the manufacturer's literature and think about the intended use of your quilt. Also, talk to experienced quilters about their favorite batting. Experiment with different battings to find which type works best for you. No matter what kind you use, before layering the batting with the quilt backing and top, unfold it and allow it to relax for several hours, or tumble it in the clothes dryer for a few minutes with no heat to remove sharp folds.

Polyester

One hundred percent polyester batting, though lightweight, is very durable and warm. It launders without shrinking and needles easily for hand quilting. One disadvantage of polyester batting is the bearding that often occurs: The fibers migrate through the fabric of the quilt top, creating a fuzzy look. Many polyester battings are bonded, or coated, to reduce bearding. Unfortunately, the bonding makes the batting a little more difficult to needle. Polyester batting comes in many different lofts, which makes it suitable for everything from quilted clothing and home accessories to puffy, tied comforters.

All-Cotton

All-cotton battings are popular with quilters who like a very flat, old-fashioned appearance, though some hand quilters think cotton is harder to needle. Unlike polyester, cotton fibers do not beard. At one time, all-cotton batting had to be quilted at very close intervals (¼ to ½ inch) to prevent lumping and migration of the fibers during washing. Some modern cotton battings can be laundered even when quilting is several inches apart. Note that cotton battings will shrink when washed. This is desirable for some quilters who want to create an antique look; the shrinking batting wrinkles the fabrics around the lines of quilting, instantly creating the look of an old quilt.

Cotton/Polyester Blends

Another option is the cotton/polyester blend batting that combines the low-loft sculpted look of cotton with the durability of polyester. This type of batting is easier to needle than the cotton and can be quilted at greater intervals. The fibers are bonded, or coated, to reduce bearding. Some quilters prefer to presoak this type of batting to break down the coating and make the needling easier. Follow the manufacturer's recommendations for pretreating.

Other Options

Keep in mind, too, that batting is not the only option. Cotton flannel gives quilts a flat look that can be ideal for miniature quilts that would be overpowered by puffy batting. Flannel may also be appropriate for items such as tablecloths and table runners, where you don't want a lot of puffiness. Quiltmakers have also used wool and silk battings.

Layering and Basting

Once your quilt top is complete and marked for quilting, your backing is prepared, and your batting is purchased, you are ready to assemble and baste together the layers. Whether you plan to hand or machine quilt, the layers must be assembled securely so that the finished quilt will lie flat and smooth.

Follow the procedure below for successful layering. If you plan to quilt by hand, baste with thread. If you will be machine quilting, use safety pins. Thread basting does not hold the layers securely enough during the machine quilting process. The thread is also more difficult to remove when quilting is completed.

For best results when thread basting large quilts, work at two or three banquet-type tables at a community center, library, or church basement. For pin basting, the best area is a large, clear area on the living room floor with carpet you can pin through when spreading out the quilt back. Whatever surface you work on, make sure it is completely free of dust and dirt before laying the quilt back on it.

Layering

1. Fold the quilt back in half lengthwise and press to form a centerline. Place the back, wrong side up, on the basting table. Position the pressed centerline at the middle of the table. To keep the backing taut, use pieces of masking tape at the corners or clamp it to the table with large binder clips from a stationery store.

2. Fold the batting in half lengthwise and lay it on the quilt backing, aligning the fold with the pressed centerline. Open out the batting; smooth and pat down any wrinkles.

3. Fold the quilt top in half lengthwise, right sides together, and lay it on the batting, aligning the fold with the center of the batting. Unfold the top; smooth it out and remove any loose threads. Make sure the backing and batting are at least 2 inches larger than the quilt top on all four sides for smaller projects. For bed-size quilts, add 3 inches extra on each side.

Basting

For hand quilting, use a long darning needle and white sewing thread to baste the layers together, making lines of basting approximately 4 inches apart. Baste from the center out in a radiating pattern, or make horizontal and vertical lines of basting in a lattice fashion, using the seams that join the blocks as guidelines.

For machine quilting, use 1-inch safety pins to secure the layers together, pinning from the center out approximately every 3 inches. Be careful not to place the pins where you intend to quilt. You may need as many as 1,000 pins to pin baste a queen-size quilt.

PIN BASTING MADE EASY

Here's an easy way to pin baste a quilt to get it ready for machine quilting. Spread the quilt backing face down on a carpeted floor. Hold the quilt back taut by pushing T-pins (sometimes called wig pins) through your quilt back and straight into the carpet. Push all the way into the backing of the carpet, pinning first along one side and then on the opposite side. Pin the remaining two sides in the same manner. Spread the batting atop the backing, followed by the quilt top. Pin layers together with 1-inch safety pins. ❖

Quilting

Most of the projects in this book are hand quilted, but a few of the wall quilts and one bed quilt are machine quilted. Whether you will be stitching by hand or by machine, the tips that follow can help with your quilting.

Hand Quilting

• Use a hoop or frame to hold the quilt layers taut and smooth during quilting.

• Use short quilting needles, called *betweens,* in either size 9 or 10.
• Use quilting thread rather than regular sewing thread.
• Start with a length of quilting thread about 18 inches long. This is long enough to keep you going for a while, but not so long that it tangles easily.
• Pop the knot through the fabric at the beginning and end of each length of thread so that no knots show on the quilt front or back. To do this, insert the needle through the top and batting about 1 inch away from where you will begin stitching. Bring the needle to the surface in position to make the first stitch. Gently tug on the thread to pop the knot through the top and bury it in the batting, as shown in **Diagram 27.**

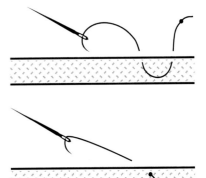

Diagram 27: Insert the needle through the top and batting, and gently tug on the thread until the knot pops through the fabric.

• Quilt by making running stitches, about $\frac{1}{16}$ to $\frac{1}{8}$ inch long, through all three layers. Try to keep the stitches straight and even.

• Thread several needles with quilting thread before you begin, and keep them handy while you work. This way you won't have to stop and thread a needle every time you finish a length of thread.

Machine Quilting

• Use a walking foot (also called an even feed foot) on your sewing machine for quilting straight lines. Use a darning or machine embroidery foot for free-motion quilting.

• To secure the thread at the beginning and end of a design, take several short stitches.

• *For free-motion quilting:* Disengage the sewing machine feed dogs so you can manipulate the quilt freely as you quilt. (Check your sewing machine manual to see how to do this.)

Choose continuous-line quilting designs so you won't have to begin and end threads as frequently as with interrupted designs.

Guide the marked design under the needle with both hands, working at an even pace so stitches will be of a consistent length.

Making and Attaching Binding

The most common edge finish for quilts is binding, cut either on the bias or on the straight of grain. Bias binding has more give, which makes it ideal for quilts that have curves or points along the outside edges. Use the yardage reserved for binding to make the type of binding you prefer. Some projects in this book have special edge finishes.

Directions for those finishes are included with the quilt projects.

French-fold binding, also called double-fold binding, is recommended for bed quilts. The bias or straight-grain binding strip is folded in half, and the raw edges are stitched to the edge of the quilt on the right side. The folded edge is then brought to the back side of the quilt, as shown in **Diagram 28,** and hand stitched in place. French-fold binding is easier to apply than single-fold binding, and its double thickness adds durability. The strips for this type of binding are cut four times the finished width plus seam allowances. As a general rule, cut the strips 2 inches wide for quilts with thin batting such as cotton and 2¼ inches wide for quilts with thicker batting. Most of the project directions in this book specify French-fold binding, and the fabric yardages are based on that type of binding.

The Pisces wallhanging (page 66) is finished with single-fold binding. To make single-fold binding, cut your fabric strips twice the width of your finished binding plus ½ inch for seam allowances. Press under ¼ inch on one long edge of the binding. This edge will be hand sewn to the back of the quilt. Stitch the other long edge of the binding to the quilt top, right sides together. Fold the binding to the quilt back and stitch in place.

The amount of binding needed for each project is included with the finishing instructions. Generally, you will need the perimeter of the quilt plus 10 to 12 inches for mitering corners and ending the binding. Three-quarters to 1 yard of fabric will usually make enough binding to finish a large quilt.

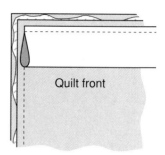

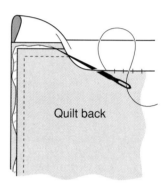

Diagram 28: For French-fold binding, fold the strip in half and stitch it to the quilt front. Bring the folded edge to the back of the quilt and hand stitch it in place.

Follow the instructions below to make continuous-cut bias binding or to join straight strips for continuous straight-grain binding. Unless the project directions tell you otherwise, sew the binding to the quilt as described below, mitering the binding at the corners.

Continuous-Cut Bias Binding

Continuous-cut bias binding is cut in one long strip from a square of fabric that has been cut apart and resewn into a tube. You must first determine the size of the square you will need. To make approximately 400 inches of 2- or 2¼-inch-wide French-fold binding, enough to bind most bed quilts, start with a 30-inch square. If you don't have enough fabric for one large square, use several smaller squares. To estimate the number of inches of binding a particular square will produce, use this formula:

Multiply the length of one side by the length of another side. Divide the result by the width of binding you want.

Using a 30-inch square and 2¼-inch binding as an example: 30 × 30 = 900; 900 ÷ 2¼ = 400 inches of binding.

Seven Steps to Continuous-Cut Binding

1. Once you have determined the size you need, measure and cut a square of fabric.

2. Fold the square in half diagonally and press lightly. Cut the square into two triangles, cutting on the fold line.

3. Place the two triangles, right sides together, as shown in **Diagram 29.** Sew the pieces together, taking a ¼-inch seam. Open out the two pieces and press the seam open. The resulting piece should look like the one shown in **Diagram 30.**

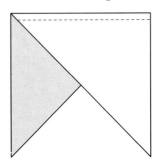

Diagram 29: Place the triangles right sides together as shown and stitch.

4. Referring to **Diagram 30,** mark cutting lines on the wrong side of the fabric in the desired binding width. Mark parallel to the bias edges.

5. Fold the fabric right sides together, bringing the two non-

bias edges together and offsetting them by one strip width, as shown in **Diagram 31.** Pin the edges together, creating a tube, and sew, taking a ¼-inch seam. Press the seam open.

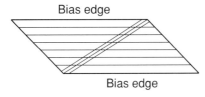

Diagram 30: Open out the two pieces and press the seam open. On the wrong side, mark cutting lines parallel to the bias edges.

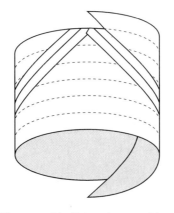

Diagram 31: Bring the non-bias edges together, offsetting them by one strip width. Sew the edges together to create a tube.

6. Cut on the marked lines, as shown in **Diagram 32,** turning the tube as you cut one long bias strip.

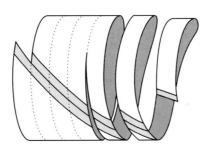

Diagram 32: Turning the tube as you go, cut along the marked lines to make one long bias strip.

7. To make French-fold binding, fold the long strip in half lengthwise, wrong sides together, and press.

Straight-Grain Binding

Straight-grain binding is a little easier to prepare than bias binding. Simply cut strips across the grain of the fabric and sew them together end to end to get the required length. Although it doesn't have the same flexibility as bias binding, it works fine for straight-edge quilts.

Simple Straight-Grain Binding Method

1. Refer to the project instructions for the amount of binding the quilt requires. Estimate and cut the needed number of strips. When possible, cut the straight strips across the width of the fabric rather than along the length so they are slightly stretchy and easier to use.

2. Join the strips as shown in **Diagram 33.** Place them right sides together, with each strip set in ¼ inch from the end of the other strip, as shown. Sew a diagonal seam. Trim the excess fabric, leaving a ¼-inch seam allowance. Continue adding strips until you have the length needed. For French-fold binding, fold and press the long strip in half lengthwise, wrong sides together.

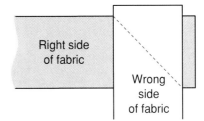

Right side of fabric

Wrong side of fabric

Diagram 33: Place the strips right sides together, positioning each strip ¼ inch in from the end of the other strip. Join with a diagonal seam.

Preparing a Quilt for Binding

Wait to trim excess batting and backing until after the binding is stitched to the top of the quilt. If the edges of the quilt are uneven after quilting, use a ruler and pencil to mark a placement line for the binding, as close as possible to the raw edges of the quilt top. This will give you a guideline against which you can align the raw edge of the binding strip. For best results, use a ruled square to mark the placement lines at the corners.

If you have a walking or even feed foot for your sewing machine, use it in place of the regular presser foot when sewing on the binding. If you do not have a walking foot, thread baste around the quilt along the edges to hold the layers firmly together during binding and to avoid puckers.

Attaching the Binding

1. Once you have made your binding strips (using either the continuous-cut bias or straight-grain strip method), you must prepare them so they can be attached to the quilt. If you are using French-fold binding, fold the long strip in half lengthwise, wrong sides together, and press. If you are using single-fold binding, you must fold over ¼ inch along one long side of the strip and press.

2. Begin attaching the binding in the middle of a side, not in a corner. Place the binding strip right sides together with the quilt top, with the raw edges of the binding strip even with the raw edge of the quilt top (or the placement line if you have drawn one).

3. Fold over the beginning raw edge of the binding approximately 1 inch, as shown in **Diagram 34.** Securing the stitches with a backstitch, begin sewing ½ inch away from the fold. Sew the binding to the quilt, stitching through all layers, ¼ inch away from the raw edge of the binding.

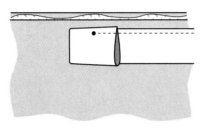

Diagram 34: Fold the raw edge back about 1 inch, and begin stitching ½ inch from the fold. Backstitch to anchor the stitching.

4. When approaching a corner, stop stitching exactly ¼ inch away from the raw edge of the corner. Backstitch and remove the quilt from the sewing machine, clipping threads.

5. Fold the binding up and away from the corner, as shown in **Diagram 35A,** forming a 45 degree angle fold.

6. Fold the binding strip back down and align the raw edges with the adjacent side of the corner, as shown in **Diagram 35B.**

7. Begin stitching the next side at the top raw edge of the quilt, as shown in **Diagram 35B.** The fold created in the fabric is essential; it provides the fullness necessary to fit around the corners as you fold the binding to the back side of the quilt. Miter all four corners in this manner.

8. As you approach the point where you began, cross the fold-ed-back beginning section with the ending section. Sew across the fold, as shown in **Diagram 36,** allowing the ending section to extend approximately ½ inch beyond the beginning.

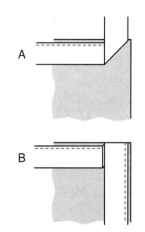

Diagram 35: Stop stitching ¼ inch from the corner and fold the binding up at a 45 degree angle (A). Fold the binding strip back down, align the raw edges with the side of the quilt top, and stitch the binding in place (B).

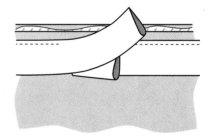

Diagram 36: Cross the beginning section with the ending section, overlapping them about ½ inch.

9. Trim away the excess batting and backing, using scissors or a rotary cutter and a ruler. Before you trim the whole quilt, trim a small section and turn the binding to the back of the quilt to determine the right amount of excess to trim. The binding will look best and wear longer if it is filled rather than hollow.

10. Turn the binding to the back of the quilt and blindstitch the folded edge in place, covering the machine stitches with the folded edge. Finish the miters at the corners by folding in the adjacent sides on the back of the quilt and placing several stitches in the miter, as shown in **Diagram 37.** Add several stitches to the miters on the front in the same manner.

If you plan to add a hanging sleeve, follow the directions below to make and attach the sleeve before turning and finishing the binding.

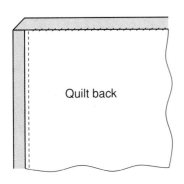

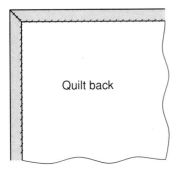

Diagram 37: Blindstitch the binding in place on the quilt back. Fold in the adjacent corner and stitch along the miter.

Adding a Hanging Sleeve

If you plan to display your quilt, at home or at a quilt show, you will certainly need to add a hanging sleeve to the back.

The best way to prepare any of the wallhangings in this book for display is to add a hanging sleeve when you are binding the quilt. A rod or dowel can be inserted in the sleeve and supported by nails or hooks on the wall. Many quilters put hanging sleeves on bed quilts as well so that their work can be exhibited at quilt shows. Use the following procedure to add a 4-inch-wide hanging sleeve, which can accommodate a 2-inch-diameter dowel or pole.

1. Cut a strip of muslin or other fabric that is 8½ inches wide and 1 inch shorter than the width of the finished quilt.

2. Machine hem the short ends. To hem, turn under ½ inch on each end of the strip and press. Turn under another ½ inch and stitch next to the pressed fold.

3. Fold and press the strip in half lengthwise, wrong sides together, aligning the two long raw edges.

4. Position the raw edges of the sleeve to align with the top raw edges on the back of the quilt, centering the sleeve on the quilt. The binding should already be sewn on the front, but not turned to the back of the quilt. Pin the sleeve in place.

5. Machine stitch the sleeve to the back of the quilt, stitching from the front by sewing on top of the stitches that hold the binding to the quilt.

6. Turn the binding to the back of the quilt and hand stitch it in place so that the binding covers the raw edge of the sleeve. (See **Diagram 38.**) When turning the binding on the edge that has the sleeve, you may need to trim away more batting and backing in order to turn the binding easily.

7. Hand stitch the bottom loose edge of the sleeve in place, being careful not to sew through to the front of the quilt.

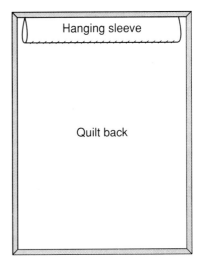

Diagram 38: Stitch the raw edge of the sleeve to the top of the quilt. Bring the binding to the back of the quilt and hand stitch it in place, covering the top raw edge of the sleeve. Then, hand stitch the bottom edge of the sleeve to the quilt back.

Directory of Quilt Shows

Because the dates and locations for many quilt shows change from year to year, and because there are new shows being added to the calendar all the time, it is impossible to provide a complete and current listing. The shows listed here are national in scope and therefore generally have fixed locations and dates. Write to the addresses provided for exact dates and complete information.

American Quilter's Society National Quilt Show and Contest

Paducah, Kentucky
Date: Generally in late April
Mailing address:
American Quilter's Society
P.O. Box 3290
Paducah, KY 42002-3290

The Great American Quilt Festival

New York City
Date: Generally in early May
Mailing address:
Museum of American Folk Art
Quilt Connection
61 West 62nd Street
New York, NY 10023

International Quilt Festival

Houston, Texas
Date: Generally the last week in October
Mailing address:
International Quilt Festival
14520 Memorial Drive #54
Houston, TX 77079

Mid-Atlantic Quilt Festival

Williamsburg, Virginia
Date: Generally the last week in February
Mailing address:
Mid-Atlantic Quilt Festival
c/o David M. & Peter J. Mancuso, Inc.
P.O. Box 667
New Hope, PA 18938

National Quilting Association

The location and date change each year for the NQA show, though it is always held during the summer.
Mailing address:
National Quilting Association
P.O. Box 393
Ellicott City, MD 21041-0393

Pacific International Quilt Festival

San Francisco, California
Date: Generally the second week in October
Mailing address:
P.I.Q.F.
c/o David M. & Peter J. Mancuso, Inc.
P.O. Box 667
New Hope, PA 18938

Quilters' Heritage Celebration

Lancaster, Pennsylvania
Date: Generally the first week in April
Mailing address:
Quilters' Heritage Celebration
P.O. Box 503
Carlinville, IL 62626

Silver Dollar City's National Quilt Festival

Branson, Missouri
Date: Generally late August or early September
Mailing address:
Special Events Department
Silver Dollar City, Inc.
West Highway 76
Branson, MO 65616